working with
karma

working with
karma

understanding and transforming your karma

Gill Farrer-Halls

First published in Great Britain in 2007 by
Godsfield Press, a division of Octopus Publishing Group Ltd
2–4 Heron Quays, London, E14 4JP

Distributed in the United States and Canada by
Sterling Publishing Co., Inc.
387 Park Avenue South, New York, NY 10016-8810

ISBN-13: 978-1-841-81316-5
ISBN-10: 1-841-81316-8

3589 5688 8/07

A CIP catalogue record for this book is available from the
British Library.

Printed and bound in China

2 4 6 8 10 9 7 5 3 1

Note

Yoga can be practised by people of all ages and states of
fitness. However, always consult a doctor if you are in doubt
about a medical condition.

contents

WHAT IS KARMA?

Karma is a deeply profound spiritual philosophy, one of the central themes of Buddhism and Hinduism. Essentially karma is one of the natural and inescapable laws of the universe, which means that we are all subject to its workings, whether or not we have heard of – or understood – the teachings on karma. It is often referred to as a kind of mystical fate or fortune, but although this definition is not entirely incorrect, the true meaning of karma is rarely realized in the modern world. This book is a simple but comprehensive introduction to the subject, and explains clearly how understanding karma can be of benefit in our lives.

Buddha Shakyamuni, the historical Buddha, is shown here seated in vajra posture, with his right leg crossed over his left. His left hand rests in the gesture of meditation, symbolizing wisdom, and holds an alms bowl, while his right hand reaches down to touch the ground, symbolizing compassionate activity.

This detail from an Indian temple shows the importance of spiritual iconography in the East.

karma: an historical perspective

For many people in the modern Western world, religion has lost much of its significance and has been replaced by a more materialistic approach to life.

When questioned about the big issues of life and death, many people say they feel that life is a one-off experience; we are born, we exist and then we die. There might be some vague idea of a Heaven or Hell to which we go after death, according to whether we have been good or bad, but there is no real sense of previous or past lives, or of how our behaviour might condition these different lives. The idea of karma is vague, and might only be referred to when something happens that it is difficult to explain.

For many people living in the East, however, karma and rebirth are much more easily accepted into their world view, because these philosophies have been embedded in the Eastern psyche since ancient times. Life and death are seen from a different perspective, and people easily accept previous and past lives and the workings of karma. Indeed, for many it is a question of what the next life will be, rather than whether there will be another incarnation. There is an implicit understanding that our actions in this life will condition the next life. From these two different perspectives it is interesting to consider how the Eastern world view arose.

the divine Vedas

Ancient history is intertwined with myths and stories that make metaphorical and metaphysical sense, rather than being literal accounts of what actually happened – which it is of course impossible to know for sure. However, there is much we can learn from the creation myths and stories of the world's different cultures. In ancient India, before Hinduism, people lived according to divine scriptures called the Vedas. The root of the word veda is *vid*, which means to know, so the word veda means knowledge – and more specifically, spiritual knowledge. The Vedas were not written down for centuries after their composition, so this knowledge was transmitted orally. The teachings and instructions contained in the Vedas are believed to have been breathed forth by the Creator as a divine gift to humankind.

The sages, or rishis, who received these divine teachings made them accessible to the wider population as spiritual guidance to live by, and they themselves also started to learn about karma. Through divine inspiration they began to understand the laws of simple, individual cause and effect. They observed that unskilful negative actions were usually caused by previous negativity, and in their turn caused further suffering. Likewise positive, skilful behaviour was usually rooted in previous skilful actions and led mostly to happiness. This fundamental basis of karma is as relevant today as it was then.

interdependence

This simple level of thinking gradually developed into abstract thought, and from abstract thinking the interdependence of all things and people was perceived. In this way the law of karma was seen to function with deeper complexity and profundity; for instance, it was observed that a whole community could be affected by the positive or negative actions of one person. However, it also became clear that other, natural forces beyond the individual were implicit in what happened in people's lives. Different gods were consequently revealed, with each one having a specific influence over destiny.

For the gods to look after the people, they needed to be honoured and propitiated, so prayers and sacrifice rituals developed. Although at first

This woman is following the principle of ahimsa and sweeping before she walks so as not to hurt any insects.

glance such rituals might seem archaic or naive, nonetheless they had – and retain – much power. Today people still pray to their gods with faith and devotion, in much the same way as these early people prayed. Sacrifice still exists, although in many cases the rituals have metamorphosed into symbolic acts, which no longer involve the harm or death of others.

the principle of ahimsa

The Jain religion that developed in India around the same time as Hinduism responded somewhat differently. Its adherents understood the working of karma in another way, and from their understanding developed the principle of ahimsa, or harmlessness. This practice forbade the harming or killing of any living being, and devout Jains still sweep their path with a soft brush before they walk, so as not to harm any little insects that might be there.

As Hinduism evolved it also partly embraced the principle of ahimsa, which still prevails today. For instance, Mahatma Gandhi's refusal to engage in violent conflict against the British colonization of India, and his espousal of non-violent resistance, was rooted in ahimsa. However, a later development in Hinduism, known as Tantra, was – and to some extent still is – rooted in elaborate rituals and sacrificial practices. Tantra also developed highly sophisticated symbolic rituals that embody the power of some of the original Vedic practices.

Tantra lies within the vast domain of yoga, which probably arose from the earliest Indian civilizations around the time of the Vedas. Some contemporary relevant yoga poses are depicted and briefly described throughout this book to demonstrate the benefits of practising yoga to gain spiritual insight and focused tranquillity. You can regard these easy-to-perform postures as a form of physical meditation that complements the sitting meditations.

the universality of karma

It is hard to pinpoint exactly when or how all of these principles, philosophies and practices evolved; it is best to regard each one as a petal of the vast flowering of Indian spirituality from the earliest times. It is beyond the scope of this book to delve deeper into these ancient mysteries. Nonetheless, it is from this melting pot of ancient religion and spiritual practice that the philosophy of karma originally evolved.

We can understand from this brief introduction that the ancient roots of karma are intimately involved with the major issues of life and death, which transcend all time periods and cultures. Early observations on how the law of karma operates, and its subsequent development into a profound and sophisticated philosophy, reveal the universal truth of karma that still affects us today.

Meditation is an ancient practice that is as helpful and beneficial for modern people as it was when it originated.

a Buddhist understanding of karma

The word karma is technically an abbreviation of the phrase 'the law of karma', which indicates first and foremost that karma is a natural and inescapable law of the universe. This means that whether or not you have heard about karma, or believe in it, nonetheless you are subject to it.

Karma is an important subject within the Buddhist canon of teachings, and it works interdependently with all the many other Buddhist teachings. So, for instance, the teachings on compassion are based on an understanding of the workings of karma. Karma is a Sanskrit word, which is also sometimes spelt kamma, the Pali equivalent. Sanskrit and Pali are both ancient Indian languages and were the original languages of Buddhism, so both words mean the same thing. However, for the sake of consistency, this book will use the Sanskrit word karma throughout.

The word karma essentially means action, but this is quite a general meaning. More specifically, we say that karma refers to actions that are willed or meant – in other words, those actions that have intention behind them. However, even if you do something instinctively, without thinking about it, there is always some level of unconscious intention. Therefore all your actions create karma, although this can be powerful or weak, depending on the different conditions influencing your individual actions. Buddhas (those who have awakened or become enlightened) are the only ones whose actions are perfectly pure and no longer generate karma.

The Sanskrit characters denoting karma. Sanskrit is the original Indian language of Buddhism.

Buddha statues are found in Nature as well as in temples and serve as a reminder of Buddhist teachings such as karma.

mental, verbal and bodily karma

A threefold division classifies karma into: mental karma that is created by the mind and thoughts; verbal karma, created through speech; and bodily karma, created through physical actions. Mental karma is the most significant, because although it exists on its own, it is also the origin of the other two types of karma. In other words, we think before we speak or physically do something – however briefly – and these thoughts influence what, and how, we say and do.

There is a further sub-classification into two types of karma: actions that are positive, skilful, beneficial and good; and actions that are negative, unskilful, harmful and bad. In the Buddhist context, skilful actions refer to those that are positive and appropriate because they have been carefully thought through and all the likely consequences have been considered.

ten negative actions

There are ten main negative actions that create bad karma. These are:

- The three physical vices of killing, stealing and sexual misconduct (such as adultery)

- The four negative acts of speech, which are lying, using words to harm others or cause conflict between them, using harsh language such as swearing, and idle gossip

- The three mental negative vices, which are covetousness, thinking ill of people, and holding wrong views (such as not believing in karma or any of the Buddha's other teachings).

ten positive actions

The ten positive counterpoint actions involve firstly giving up these negative actions and then cultivating their positive opposites. Therefore they are:

- The three physical virtues of protecting life, being generous to others, and responsible sexual behaviour

- The four positive acts of speech, which are being truthful, creating harmony and reconciliation among others, talking pleasantly, and having useful, meaningful conversations

- The three mental virtues, which are being content with what you have, being kind to others, and developing the conviction that what Buddha taught is beneficial to yourself and others.

Negative karma arises from actions that are fuelled by ignorance and delusion; desire, avarice and attachment; and aversion, hatred and anger. In Buddhism these are called the Three Poisons. They represent the negative qualities that keep us trapped in samsara, the cycle of birth and rebirth that we escape only by attaining enlightenment. Positive karma arises from actions that are not ignorance, not desire and not aversion. You might think it would be easier and quicker to say that positive karma arises from wisdom, love and renunciation. However, it is traditional in Buddhism to describe the positive qualities as being in direct opposition to the Three Poisons, because this acts as a reminder to us of what they are and how to avoid them.

For an action to be considered fully complete, three stages must occur. These are the motivation to perform the action, the successful fulfilment of the action, and the satisfaction of completing the action. If only one or two stages of an action are fulfilled, then the karma created is less, while a fully completed action generates greater karmic consequences. For example, if you mistakenly squash an insect and feel genuinely sorry that you killed it, then only the action itself has occurred; there was no intention or satisfaction involved. The karmic consequences are therefore considerably less than if you had the intention and deliberately jumped on the insect, and then felt happy and satisfied that you had successfully killed it.

the law of cause and effect

Karma is also known as the 'law of cause and effect'. Essentially this means that every action, however tiny or seemingly insignificant, creates a cause for an eventual result, which is called the fruit of the action. Most of our actions and their consequences are complex and are influenced by hundreds of little factors throughout our lives – and throughout many different lifetimes – that intermingle in a complex web. So often you cannot clearly see how karma operates; a leading Tibetan Buddhist teacher has described karma as being the hardest of all the Buddhist teachings to understand fully. We will consider the law of cause and effect in more detail in the next chapter (see page 34).

A further classification of karma is according to what results are achieved from what actions. The first category is called 'black karma, black result'

This striking and unusual image shows well the diversity and richness of Buddhist iconography.

and includes all harmful actions of body, speech and mind. 'White karma, white result' incorporates all non-harmful and virtuous actions. 'Black and white karma, black and white result' includes actions that are partly harmful, partly not. An example of this type of action would be telling a lie in order not to hurt someone's feelings. Although the intention is positive, the act itself is not, so the karmic consequences will be mixed.

karma neither black nor white

The last category needs further explanation: this is karma that is neither black nor white, result neither black nor white. This category arises when our underlying intention is to transcend the other kinds of karma altogether by trying to awaken, or become enlightened – the ultimate

goal of Buddhism. This brings us to the main purpose of practising
Buddhism, which is to avoid suffering and to find happiness. An immediate
response might be that creating karma that brings happiness as its result is
surely the best thing to do – after all, you have just read that the main
purpose of pract·   ddhism is to find happiness. However, Buddhism
teaches that   erything is impermanent, so even if you create
the ca·   sulting happiness cannot last forever. Sooner
or ·   happiness will be exhausted and you will
                      · highest aspiration must be to transcend
                      ds enlightenment.

                         ·hing very clear: it is we ourselves
                         ·throughout our lives. The person
                          ed the causes for a pleasant life
                            ·es. Those who suffer illness,
                             ·uses for their unpleasant
b·   ·n previous lives. Most
po·   ·ces throughout their
exper·
people
lives, refl·   ·n earlier lives.

the path to   nt

By now it should be   ·r that karma is not fatalistic. By consciously trying
to act with wisdom, kindness and compassion for others as much as
possible, you will create the karma for positive rebirths in which you will
experience happiness and the opportunity to create further good karma.
Such virtuous behaviour will eventually lead those who follow this path
beyond karma altogether, to enlightenment.

This is a brief introduction to the Buddhist understanding of karma. In the
following chapters you will have the opportunity to examine in greater
depth how karma operates and affects your life. For instance, in one
chapter you can learn about how your job and career choices might affect
your karma, and in another chapter you can explore the relationship
between wealth and karma. There are many practical suggestions and
exercises on working with karma, as well as different meditations and
rituals to try. Once you begin to understand the profound nature of
karma and how it operates in your life, you will discover a path that can
lead you towards a happier existence.

a meditation on karma

This meditation gives you the opportunity to witness the arising and passing of thoughts and feelings. Because these are conditioned by habitual instincts, observing them gives you a glimpse into how karma operates in the mind.

1 Sit comfortably with your back straight. Close your eyes and bring your attention to your breath. Observe how one exhalation causes and conditions the next inhalation. For instance, if you take a particularly deep breath in, the next out-breath will be equally deep. Even with normal breathing, each inhalation causes an exhalation.

2 Observe your current state of mind. What thoughts and feelings are flickering through it? Simply observe them arising and passing; don't judge them. Try to ascertain if a thought was caused by previous thoughts, and note how it might act as a cause for future thoughts. For instance, thinking, 'It's a nice sunny day today' might lead to reflecting on memories of previous sunny days, or to fantasies of a future holiday. Contemplate how your thoughts condition one another in this way.

3 Now bring to mind a habitual negative tendency; for example, perhaps you often feel angry. Investigate why this might be. Perhaps your mind is familiar with feelings of anger from previous occasions, so it is easy for your mind to become angry now. The anger is self-perpetuating; it causes you – and others – suffering now, and creates the karma for you to feel anger again. Determine to break this karmic cycle. Promise yourself that next time you feel anger starting, you will breathe deeply and let it go. After a few times of not indulging your anger, you will notice that you don't tend to feel angry so easily.

4 Begin to trace your past mental experiences, starting with earlier today and going back days, weeks and years. Don't get caught in reminiscences; the objective is to understand how thoughts and feelings have a cause and an effect. For instance, recollecting a sad, painful memory might make you feel hurt now, even though there is nothing in the present to cause you to feel sad.

5 Ask yourself, 'Are these old thoughts part of who I am now? Did they condition who I have become?'

6 Reflect that your personality and experiences in this life are conditioned by the karma from previous existences. Although at death your personality – the 'I' sense you feel – dies, nonetheless the karma it created will go on to shape the personality of the next life.

7 Return to watching the breath, noticing how each inhalation causes an exhalation in an endless cycle. Take a few quiet moments to reflect on your meditation before moving on with your daily life.

how to do mountain pose

Practising Tadasana, or mountain pose, helps induce meditative awareness. The hands held in the prayer position at the heart are a gesture of reverence towards the Divine. The pose grounds and centres both mind and body.

1 Stand with your feet together, feeling your soles rooted to the earth. Raise the front of your body slightly and lean into the back of your body. Extend your fingers and keep your head straight for several seconds, breathing steadily.

2 Now inhale and bring your palms together. As you exhale, release any tension. When you feel calm and balanced, close your eyes and maintain the pose for a few breaths.

debunking myths: what karma isn't

Because karma is an Eastern spiritual philosophy, Westerners are sometimes confused about what karma is exactly, or what it means in our lives.

Contemporary phrases such as 'cosmic karma' are meaningless, and the joke 'Your karma ran over my dogma' (although amusing on first hearing) also has no real meaning. However, these phrases clearly demonstrate that the word has entered the English language – even if it is often used incorrectly. It is therefore interesting and worthwhile to explore why these misconceptions about karma have arisen.

Perhaps the most fundamental misconception is that karma refers to some kind of mystical fate or fortune of the 'cosmic karma' kind. This idea of fate, fortune or destiny relies upon the belief that there is either a God or gods who exert control over humankind, or that humans live in a random, meaningless world where anything can and will happen. In ancient Greek and Roman mythology, for instance, there is frequent reference to how the whims of the gods often had devastating effects on the lives of certain humans.

creating your own karma

This idea of karma as fate is quite different from the way non-theistic Asian religions interpret karma. From the Buddhist perspective, each individual is understood to be responsible for his or her actions and, in a general way, this belief can be summed up as 'you reap what you sow'. The key notion here is personal responsibility for your own actions. Unlike the Judaeo-Christian religions, which posit an omnipotent, omniscient Creator God who can affect the destiny of individuals through divine intervention, in Buddhism you create your own karma. There is no God who can forgive negative actions, or punish you for them; the actions themselves condition your experience.

Another common misperception occurs when the word karma is used to mean some kind of luck. For instance, a string of unfortunate events happens to a person and someone says, 'All these terrible things happened

According to the Buddhist teachings each one of us is responsible for our own actions and the karma they create.

to her; what bad luck, it must be her karma.' It may indeed be her karma, but the sequence of unfortunate events that she suffered has nothing to do with luck. When you think about it, everyone you know has suffered some misfortune in their lives, but some good things have also happened to everyone. This is the nature of life: highs and lows, good times and bad, health and sickness, births and deaths – these events happen to us all throughout our lives, although it may well seem that some people have more good times than bad, and vice versa.

different perceptions

When you take a look at the outer circumstances of people's lives in this way, it is easy to make judgements instinctively about what you find. But not everyone sees things in the same light, and what you perceive as misfortune, someone else might perceive as the opposite. For example, if you hear that your friend has lost his well-paid job, you might think this will cause him deprivation, suffering and unhappiness. However, another friend on hearing this news will think how lucky he is to be free of his job; he will have more time, less stress and will feel healthier. Your perception of external events, and the way you relate to them, affects your karma.

Shopping can become a habit that keeps you trapped in an endless cycle of desire and dissatisfaction.

From the Buddhist perspective, we all share the same fundamental nature, the natural wish to be happy and not to suffer. Actions leading to happiness are considered to be positive and virtuous, while actions leading to suffering are considered negative and non-virtuous. We spend much of our lives trying to attain objects and experiences that we think will make us happy, and avoiding those that cause suffering. So we work towards acquiring a nice home, a satisfying career, a loving husband or wife, children, holidays, possessions and so on. However, no sooner do we satisfy our current desires than we find we want more, different, newer things to keep us happy. It seems something is not quite right in this way of pursuing happiness.

the endless cycle of desire

Because the wish for happiness is our major preoccupation, we need to examine the real karmic causes of happiness and suffering. When we do not have the things we desire, we crave them endlessly, and this causes suffering. Likewise, when we have things or experiences we don't want, we get caught up in negative thoughts about how much we dislike the situation, and this aversion causes suffering. When we do obtain the thing we desired, we are satisfied for a while, but before long we are bored with our new possession, or the effect of a pleasant experience wears off so that we want to repeat it. Desire then arises again, and while it remains unfulfilled we are dissatisfied. Therefore we can conclude that satisfying our desires does not bring real, lasting happiness. It simply keeps us trapped in an endless cycle of desire and dissatisfaction.

Real, lasting happiness arises from eliminating desire for the things we like, and aversion to things we don't like. This doesn't mean that it is wrong or bad to want to have nice things, nor should we turn away from them if they come our way. We should certainly enjoy them for as long as they last. However, we need to realize that desire itself is the obstacle that prevents us finding true happiness and keeps us dissatisfied. In this way we can enjoy pleasant experiences and new possessions, but not be obsessive about having them, or disappointed when they cease to give us pleasure. When unpleasant things arise, or we don't get what we want, we can try to accept this, and reflect that all things are impermanent and that sooner or later the suffering will change.

a ritual to free yourself of selfish thinking

Practising this ritual can help you lessen – and eventually eliminate – selfish thinking. It will help you cultivate generosity and realize that the true essence of giving is a generous spirit, together with actual acts of giving.

When you give something to someone with no expectation of gratitude, or a return gift, then the person receiving the gift also receives the spirit of generosity. Giving is not dependent on wealth. Even if you are materially poor, there are things you can give. Time is a precious commodity in the contemporary world, and giving someone the gift of your time can be an act of real generosity. Giving your time to others involves listening. In the same way that a material gift given carelessly is rooted in selfish thinking, if you do not give your full attention to others when listening to them, this is also selfish.

Receiving is an integral part of giving, and you can try to be skilful in the way you receive gifts from others. Even if you are given something you don't want or like, try to be gracious in receiving it and thank the person wholeheartedly. By accepting their gift courteously and appreciating their kindness, you have given that person an opportunity to practise generosity.

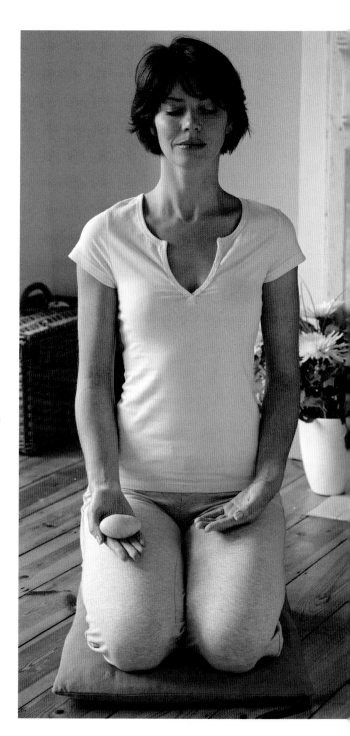

1 Find a quiet place and make sure you have 20 minutes of free time. Sit comfortably and spend a few minutes reflecting on how you would like to lessen your selfish thoughts and actions. Ask yourself, 'If I am stingy towards myself, how can I be truly generous towards others?' You need to learn how to be giving to yourself as a first step towards lessening selfish thinking.

2 Take a small everyday object such as a stone. Hold it in your right hand and notice what it feels like to have the stone. Try to feel a real appreciation for having and holding it. Reflect that a small, inexpensive gift given purely with love creates more happiness for the giver and receiver than an expensive gift given resentfully, or with the expectation of receiving something in return.

3 Slowly transfer the stone from your right hand to your left hand. Feel that your right hand is giving the stone to your left hand. Remain conscious and aware of the sensation of giving. At the same time, your left hand is receiving the stone. Develop a feeling of appreciation that you are receiving something. Although the stone has no material value, try to experience the sensation of giving and receiving something with a true and pure spirit of generosity.

4 Continue to transfer the stone back and forth between your hands slowly for ten minutes. Observe your feelings, noticing how they change.

5 Reflect that practising this ritual will help you to give and receive more authentically, and will eventually lessen selfish thinking.

western ideas relevant to karma: dreamwork and mediumship

Although karma is a spiritual philosophy from the East, because it is described as being a universal law, there are Western traditions, philosophies and practices that are relevant to the truths of karma.

In one way the truths of karma are easy to perceive; we can all see simple examples of cause and effect surrounding us in daily life. On a more complex level, we all experience an immediate karmic result from our actions in the way we remember them. For example, if you tell a lie, once the act is over and done with, a memory remains of having told a falsehood, and that memory is the karmic result. Because you know it is wrong to tell lies, the memory of telling one is unpleasant in some way. So if you told a lie that caused others great suffering, remembering the lie and its consequences is likely to cause you suffering too. On the other hand, whenever you do something kind, generous or compassionate, the memory of this considerate action will make you feel happy.

Dreamwork – the deliberate recollection and analysis of your dreams on a regular basis – is an interesting way of considering karma. The times before going to sleep and waking up exist on the threshold of changing levels of consciousness. We are all familiar with the sensation of not quite having fallen asleep and not quite being fully awake, and if we can maintain awareness of what we are experiencing during these times we can learn something of how our minds work. However, what actually happens to our mind and consciousness when we fall asleep and dream is truly amazing! Going to sleep is even sometimes called *le petit mort*, or 'little death', because we lose consciousness, although because it happens to us regularly we tend to take this extraordinary state for granted.

keeping a dream journal

It is often said that dreams are the unconscious trying to bring issues through into waking consciousness. Because dreams exist on a different level from waking consciousness, we tend to forget them soon after

Dreams can be regarded as karmic imprints from previous actions that perhaps still need some conscious thought and resolution.

waking, so writing them down immediately in a dream journal is a good way to remember them. After noting your dreams down, spending the next ten minutes or so reflecting on their content may give you insights into what your unconscious is trying to tell you. The surreal language of dreams is not always obvious or immediately accessible, but with practice you can learn to interpret your dreams over time. In a similar way to memory functioning as the karmic result of our actions, dreams can also be regarded as some kind of karmic imprints, particularly those that the unconscious is telling us need some resolution.

Dreams are deeply personal, and you need to use your own analysis alongside the classic interpretations of images that you can find in dream dictionaries. Once you have developed some idea of your dream language, you may well discover a narrative gradually emerging from the apparently random chaos of images and events. Noting recurrent symbols and patterns can help you discover what your unconscious psychological life is trying to communicate to you. For instance, you might find an underlying theme of recurrent fear in a sequence of dreams. If you regard this fear as a negative karmic imprint from some past unskilful action, then you can work to transform it so that it loses its power over you. This can be a positive way of dealing with painful karmic imprints.

Writing your dreams down regularly in a dream journal helps you notice recurring symbols and patterns in your dreams.

mediumship

In a rather different way, mediumship is also relevant to karma. Mediums are spirit messengers who have the unusual gift of being able to communicate messages to the living from the spirit world. Authentic mediums also practise spiritual healing, because those they work with are commonly the recently bereaved, who experience huge suffering. Mediums bring much comfort and healing to the people who come to them, alongside the messages they communicate from the spirit world.

Although those who do not believe in any kind of life after death dispute the authenticity of mediumship, scientific tests and experiments have demonstrated beyond reasonable doubt that a few gifted people do seem able genuinely to communicate messages from the spirit world. True mediums are usually those who refuse to charge money for their services, and who stress the spiritual healing aspect of their work. In this way they seek only to be of benefit to others and are not interested in personal financial gain or fame.

unfinished business

Sometimes with bereavement there is sense of unfinished business between the deceased and someone who was very close to that person – usually, but not always, a father, mother, daughter, son, wife or husband. This sense of 'unfinished business' can be seen as a karmic relationship that perhaps did not have the chance to fulfil its destiny in this lifetime. Often the person died suddenly and unexpectedly in an accident; sometimes there are unresolved issues between the two people. Whatever the reason, if a person feels the need to communicate with someone after his or her death, then a medium can help.

The idea of karma is intricately intertwined with rebirth, so communication from the spirit world seems logical, as both karma and mediumship are based on some form of life after death. Communicating messages from the Other Side brings the bereaved comfort and can help them accept the passing of their loved one. Part of this healing process is also about helping to resolve the karmic relationship by assisting the bereaved to let go of their attachment to the deceased, which allows both the bereaved and the deceased to move on.

creating an altar for meditation

A personal altar gives you a point of focus for meditating on karma. Creating an altar is a devotional act that helps generate a contemplative frame of mind and a tranquil ambience in which to meditate. Your altar, together with the offerings you place upon it, becomes a sacred space that acts as a conduit between the mundane and spiritual worlds.

The best place to create your altar is in a quiet, private room where you can meditate on karma in tranquillity and without interruptions. A low table, shelf or mantelpiece is suitable for an altar. You should be able to sit comfortably in front of your altar on a chair, or on a cushion on the floor. Clean your altar before placing anything on it. You might also like to cover the surface with a beautiful cloth.

offerings to the Divine

Everything you place on your altar becomes an offering to the Divine and to your own spiritual potential for understanding karma. So your offerings should be pure and beautiful and should hold spiritual meaning for you. Because karma is part of the Buddhist tradition, it is appropriate to place a statue of Buddha or a picture of a Buddhist teacher in the centre. If you are Christian or belong to another faith, you can use any image that helps you connect with your spiritual path, such as a painting of a saint. Traditional altar offerings include candles, incense, a bowl of water and fresh flowers. These can be offered each time you meditate. Arrange your chosen offerings around the central image in an aesthetic arrangement to inspire your meditation.

You should also place a symbol of karma upon your altar. For example, a pair of dice might remind you that you engage in an act of free will when you choose to roll them, but that the result is up to chance, fate or predetermination. Alternatively, you could find a picture of a stone being thrown into water, which shows ripples spreading outwards in ever-increasing circles; this image is a reminder that all our actions reverberate extensively, with many different effects and consequences (see page 32).

a simple meditation on karma

1 Sit comfortably with your back straight. Close your eyes and take a couple of deep breaths.

2 Bring to mind a habitual negative tendency, such as often feeling impatient. Consider that perhaps you tend to feel impatient quickly because your mind is familiar with impatience.

3 Reflect that previous impatience acts as a cause for current impatient feelings, and that current impatience acts as a cause for impatience to arise in the future.

4 Resolve to break this karmic cycle of impatience. Reflect that impatience serves no useful purpose and only causes distress. Promise yourself that next time you will try to let go of the impatient feelings by taking a few deep breaths instead to calm yourself.

HOW DOES KARMA WORK?

In Buddhism the operation of karma is classically demonstrated with the analogy of throwing a stone into a pond. When the stone is thrown in, it has the effect of creating ripples that spread outwards till they reach the far edges of the pond. This then causes the ripples to spread back to their cause, the stone – and the stone is then subjected to pressure from the ripples. In the same way our actions reverberate outwards and eventually, when the appropriate conditions arise, the results come back and we feel their effect.

Vajrasattva, meaning hero of indestructible reality, is the Buddha of purification. Practising visualization meditation on Vajrasattva, and reciting his mantra, helps to purify your body, speech and mind and is especially effective in transforming anger and hatred. In this way Vajrasattva is particularly important in helping to dispel negative karma and increase positive karma.

Considering others to be as precious as yourself and helping them unselfishly is skilful behaviour that creates good karma.

cause and effect

Karma is often called the law of cause and effect, or the law of causality. Causality works in a sophisticated way, beyond the simplicity of 'good actions cause good results' and 'bad actions cause bad results'.

Although it is technically correct that good actions cause good results, it is important to understand that karma operates in a complex way over many lifetimes. For example, suppose you see someone who has lived a good life, and who has been kind and generous to others, experience suffering later in life. The law of karma states unequivocally that this person must have acted at some point in a way to cause this suffering. Therefore you can assume that it must have been in a previous life that this person acted badly, but that he or she is only now experiencing the consequences in this life.

intention before action

We create karma with our body, speech and mind. Mind (or thought) is the most important of these three because it is the most prolific; we have intention before we act and we have many thoughts that do not lead to physical actions. According to the law of cause and effect, skilful, positive and good thoughts are of benefit to the mind and psyche, while unskilful, negative and bad thoughts are harmful. In this way, cultivating positive thoughts creates the cause for experiencing a happy, calm and peaceful state of mind.

It is helpful to consider what effects your words and actions will have before you speak and act, so that you can avoid speaking or acting in ways that will cause you future suffering. A seemingly well-intentioned action can be spoilt by ulterior motives, or by negative mind-states such as anger or hatred. So it is important to check your intention before you do something, to ensure that the effects of both the intention and the action will be positive.

skilful behaviour

A common error is to regard the law of cause and effect as a kind of spiritual bank account, with credits of good actions and debits of bad actions. This line of thought supposes that you can perform good deeds now, as an investment for your future. However, because this thought is based on selfishness, the karma accrued will have mixed consequences. A more positive way to act is to avoid unskilful actions and cultivate skilful ones, because you understand that this causes happiness not only for yourself, but for others too. When you consider others to be as precious as yourself, and act unselfishly, this skilful behaviour creates good karma.

Simply having the intentions for good actions is not enough; you need to develop these good intentions into positive actions. In other words, if you want happiness, you must first create the causes. It is also important to consider what effects your actions will have before you do them, so that you can avoid actions that may cause suffering for yourself or others.

a visualization meditation to cherish others

This visualization meditation on exchanging self for others is a powerful antidote to self-cherishing, and a stimulus for developing love and compassion for others. This is one of the more powerful practices to help reduce negative karma (by lessening self-cherishing) and intensify positive karma (by increasing the cherishing of others). Although the practice is done in the mind as a meditation, with regular practice your own behaviour will also transform.

1 Sit comfortably with your back straight. Close your eyes and bring your attention to your breath. Observe your breathing for a few minutes to calm the mind.

2 Think about how you and others are equal. Reflect that all beings want happiness and to avoid suffering; you are no different from anyone else. As you and others are equal in this way, consider the foolishness of cherishing yourself above others; realize that their needs are just as important as yours.

3 Contemplate the foolishness of self-cherishing. Consider that by selfishly looking only after yourself and neglecting others, you will increase your suffering by creating negative karma. Reflect that all beings are interdependent. Self-cherishing can never lead to happiness, because true happiness cannot exist while those around you are still suffering.

4 Contemplate the wisdom of cherishing others. Consider that by looking after others before caring for yourself, you will increase your happiness by creating positive karma. Reflect on the happiness you feel when you have helped others.

5 Reflect that in the past you have ignored the needs of others through self-cherishing, and that now you wish to exchange self-cherishing for cherishing others. Say to yourself, 'I used to ignore others, but from now on I shall consider their needs as more important than my own.' Repeat this phrase under your breath a few times.

6 Contemplate the huge amount of others' suffering, compared to the tiny quantity of your own suffering. Resolve that you would like to take away their suffering, and say to yourself, 'I shall endeavour to remove all suffering from all beings.' Generate compassion for all beings, and feel how their suffering is unbearable. Visualize all their suffering becoming rays of black smoke that dissolve into the self-cherishing in your heart. Feel that your self-cherishing has lessened and that you have tried to lessen the suffering of others.

7 Contemplate how you would like to help others to be happy. Say to yourself, 'May I give my happiness and virtue to others, and may all beings have happiness.' Generate love for all beings and wish them happiness. Visualize replicas of yourself emanating from your heart and reaching out to help others in whatever way they need. Feel that your self-cherishing has lessened and that you have tried to increase the happiness of others. Finally, dedicate the merit from this practice to the benefit of all beings.

how to do tree pose

Vrikshasana, or tree pose, is a balancing pose that helps develop physical and mental equilibrium.

1 Stand with your feet slightly apart and focus on your breathing. Raise your right knee to your chest, then swing the knee round and slightly down till the sole of your right foot rests on your left inner calf or thigh. Bring your hands together in the prayer position.

2 Focus on an object in front of you to maintain your balance. When you feel focused and balanced raise your hands above your head, concentrating on your breathing. Hold the pose for a few moments or as long as is comfortable.

individual, collective and universal karma

So far we have considered individual karma, but it is clear that we do not live in isolation from each other; we live interdependently and cooperatively in the family, in small communities and within larger society. This means that, to some degree on a social level, we share karma, so we are involved in creating and experiencing the results of collective karma as well as our own individual karma.

On the widest level, all beings living on our planet Earth share universal karma. Although the implications of universal karma would be fascinating, it is extremely difficult to consider the vast, cosmic context in which universal karma operates. However, it is fruitful and interesting to take a look at how collective karma functions.

collective karma

Collective karma is created through intention, in the same way as individual karma. Society instigates laws and social conventions as a way of regulating collective human behaviour. This is necessary because human actions are often motivated by the selfish desire for personal gain at the expense of others. Without laws governing exploitative behaviour, personal ambition for wealth would lead to negative actions. However, sometimes those in power also operate from the desire for material gain rather than from a sense of civic duty, and then problems arise.

For instance, the indiscriminate dumping of toxic waste creates a danger for the environment and for public health. Therefore the government creates laws regulating how these toxins are to be disposed of. However, those in charge of running the industries that create toxic waste are not inclined to minimize their profits, and are prepared to spend only a tiny amount on waste disposal. They may find ways to circumvent the laws, and find government officials prepared to collude. Such short-sighted behaviour is motivated by greed and creates collective negative karma, alongside health problems and environmental destruction.

true happiness

Such damaging behaviour is caused by the fundamental error of believing that happiness is to be found in an abundance of material goods and the acquisition of wealth. There is often a disregard for the environment, in the mistaken belief that humankind does not exist interdependently with the environment. Because true happiness lies beyond materialism, this is an example of wrong view causing wrong action, and the resulting collective karma experienced by society at large is therefore negative.

On the other hand, when a group of people are guided by good qualities, their actions have beneficial effects. So when people act collectively through kindness and compassion, positive and beneficial actions are undertaken. For example, international human-aid organizations relieve much suffering in the world and create collective good karma.

This overall mix of negative and positive collective behaviour results in mixed collective karma, and we see societies experiencing some problems, but also working towards their resolution.

free will or destiny?

The timeless philosophical debate about whether we are subject to the vagaries of destiny, or create our own fate through free will, is intimately connected with karma. You have already read that we are all responsible for our actions, so it seems from a karmic perspective that we have free will. However, life is not as simple as this 'either/or' debate.

If you become impatient while waiting for the morning bus this will affect your mood adversely for the whole day.

Although it is true that we create our karmic destiny through the way we act, nonetheless the circumstances in which we find ourselves also play a role. Consider the following example.

karmic habits

Imagine that you are someone who becomes impatient waiting for the bus. Your usual response is to become increasingly agitated and worried about being late. Reflecting on how karma operates can help change your stressful reactions, which only cause you suffering and cannot alter the circumstances. If you accept that the situation is beyond your control and it is not your fault that the journey might make you late, then you can relax. If you remain stressed and angry, you will only cause further suffering to yourself and others by expressing your irritation.

Changing your reactions and feelings is not easy; they are mental and emotional karmic habits that have accumulated and strengthened over this life and previous lifetimes. They cannot be altered overnight. You cannot force these changes; they need to happen naturally because you have amended the way you think. Consider the cause and effect of the above situation. Has anything in your behaviour caused it, such as being late yourself for the bus? If you did anything that contributed to the cause, then you need to accept it and resolve not to do it again. If circumstances seem to have conspired against you, then you must accept that too.

impatience as a cause of suffering

The feelings of impatience and irritation may be causing you suffering, but recognizing that you don't want to suffer is an important step towards eliminating it. If you consider your negative feelings and recognize that they only cause you suffering, then you can change them. Reflect upon a past occasion when you missed the bus. Perhaps you were feeling so angry by the time you arrived at work late that you ended up in an argument, which exacerbated your suffering and caused someone else to suffer too.

Realizing how negative feelings are pointless, and damaging, helps those feelings begin to lessen. Reflect that in the whole vastness of life, one little incident of being late is insignificant. Seeing the situation in this way will help transform your anger into a calmer state, so that you don't fall prey to negative emotions all the time. Accepting the unpleasant things in life, without reacting badly to them, enables you to take responsibility for creating your own happiness, despite troublesome circumstances.

rebirth and karma

Most of our actions create karmic consequences that are not experienced immediately, and so karmic fruition is divided into three categories: that experienced at some point during this lifetime; that experienced in the next lifetime; and that experienced in other, future lives.

The Buddhist scriptures indicate that the majority of our actions will bear fruit in future lives. So when we witness kind, generous people suffering in this life, we can rest assured they will eventually experience the positive karmic consequences of their good actions in a later life. Karma and rebirth are therefore deeply interlinked.

Lighting a new candle from one about to go out shows the transference of energy from one object to another.

karmic imprints

What exactly is rebirth? The Buddhist texts illustrate rebirth with an analogy: the flame of a dying candle is used to light a new candle and then peters out. The new candle is alight, but is it the same flame? It is neither the same nor a different flame; there has simply been a transference of energy from one object to another. Only the subtlest consciousness goes from one life to the next – the individual person, with their personality and characteristics, is extinguished at death. This subtle consciousness carries with it all the karma created in the life just finished, together with any karma from previous lives that has not yet come to fruition. These karmic imprints determine the quality of the next life, and some of the karma carried over will also come to fruition in this next life when it meets the appropriate conditions.

According to traditional Buddhist teachings, certain behaviour creates specific karmic consequences. A person who easily finds wealth and prosperity in this life created the cause by being generous in a previous existence. Someone who dies young in this life created the cause by killing or not protecting others in a previous life. Beauty is the result of pure ethical behaviour in a past life, while people who find it difficult to express themselves, or who are not believed or taken seriously in this life, created the cause by lying in a previous existence. We can see from these examples that karma is interlinked with responsible, ethical behaviour – in other words, we reap what we sow.

karma and talent

Rebirth is quite a difficult idea in Western culture, even though some early Christian sects believed in a form of rebirth. However, reflecting on the phenomenon of talent can help you understand karma passing from one life to the next. For instance, those with outstanding musical talent often describe their ability as if they already knew how to play music when they first started. People as diverse as Mozart and Bob Dylan learnt music very quickly from an early age and had an inner sense of harmony and rhythm. This can be seen as musical training in a previous life creating karma for the musical ability to be carried over to a new life.

Musical talent can be explained as musical training in a previous life creating karma for musical ability in the next life.

a meditation on the Buddha

The Sanskrit word Buddha means 'fully awakened one', and refers not only to the historical Buddha, but to all beings that awaken to their true nature, become perfect and no longer create karma. These enlightened beings can manifest in different ways to offer us love, wisdom and compassion and to help us awaken too. Every living being has Buddha nature: the inherent ability to attain enlightenment and realize the fundamental pure nature of mind.

Of course attaining enlightenment is not easy! But meditating on the Buddha helps you identify with the pure qualities he represents. In this way the qualities of an enlightened being will gradually begin to manifest in your own mind. This meditation on the Buddha is a powerful way to generate good karma. Practised regularly, it will enable your mind to become more open to love, compassion and wisdom, and less inclined to anger, attachment and hatred.

You will need a picture of the Buddha, or other enlightened spiritual figure such as Jesus, to help you visualize their pure qualities.

1 Sit comfortably with your back straight. Close your eyes and bring your attention to your breath. Observe your breathing for a few minutes to calm the mind.

2 Reflect that this meditation on the Buddha will not only help you generate good karma, but that by working towards your own enlightenment you will be of benefit to others, to help relieve them of suffering and experience happiness.

3 Buddha's face is radiantly beautiful, full of love and peace. His compassionate smile looks out at you and all other beings with no judgement or criticism; he accepts you fully just as you are.

4 Visualize rays of light radiating from Buddha's heart in an endless stream. These rays are full of miniature emanations of Buddha, which reach out to help all beings everywhere. Feel the rays of light reach you, and your heart opens to receive his compassion. You feel blessed and calm, full of joy.

5 Feel the living presence of Buddha. Reflect upon his pure, awakened qualities and his willingness and ability to help you become free of negativities and cultivate skilful qualities that will enable you to generate good karma.

6 Mentally request the Buddha to bless you, to help you be free of all your negative qualities and develop the positive qualities that will lead you towards enlightenment.

7 Accepting your request, the Buddha emanates from his heart a stream of pure white light that reflects all his pure, enlightened qualities. The light pours into your own body through the crown of your head and fills you with pure white light.

8 You feel full of bliss. Rest in this state for a few minutes before moving on with your daily life.

Meditating on the serene and benevolent features of the Buddha's face is an inspiration to act with love, wisdom and compassion.

a meditation on patience

Impatience, irritation and anger are the usual responses when things don't happen the way we would like them to. The ego wants things its own way immediately and, when thwarted, the response is frustration of some kind. Anger and other negative emotions arise that often lead to unskilful actions that create bad karma.

Meditating on patience is a powerful way to transform the negative thoughts and behaviour that cause bad karma. However, remember that dealing with negative emotions is hard work; practising patience is a gradual step towards transforming bad karma, not an instant magical solution.

1 Sit comfortably with your back straight. Close your eyes and bring your attention to your breath. Observe your breathing for a few minutes to calm the mind.

2 Consider that impatience and other negative emotions are not inherently evil; they sometimes arise naturally in the mind and you should not feel ashamed when this happens. Instead, try to regard impatience as an impermanent feeling, but contemplate that it is unskilful to act impatiently. Realize that the feeling will pass.

3 Reflect that the impatient feeling is not you; it is a fleeting emotion passing through your mind. If you do not identify with the impatience and can see it as a deluded, negative mind-state rather than an integral part of your being, it is easier to let the feeling go.

4 You are powerless to stop things going wrong in life, and this is inherently unsatisfactory. But if you accept the situation and deal with it patiently, it creates far less suffering than if you act badly. Ask yourself why you fight difficult circumstances when this only makes things worse.

5 Try to see that a current difficult situation is like a dream. Although the situation seems all too real in the present moment, in a few days when the negative feelings have passed, it will seem a faded, distant memory. So reflect that there is no point in acting unskilfully and creating the cause for future suffering.

6 Remember cause and effect: if a difficult situation has arisen now, then at some point in the past – even in a life a long time ago – a cause was created for the difficulty to manifest. If you behave patiently, accept the situation and do your best not to make things worse, then the negative karma will be purified.

7 Consider that difficult situations offer you a way to develop spiritually by giving you the chance to practise patience, instead of reacting negatively and creating bad karma. Transforming the way you feel about difficult situations in this way makes them much easier to deal with.

8 Return to watching your breath for a few minutes. Take a few quiet moments to reflect on your meditation before moving on with your daily life.

A mandala is a Tibetan symbol of the divine abode of a deity, represented as a square palace within circular protection wheels. It symbolizes the complete reorientation of experience brought about by awakening. The intricacy and profound nature of the mandala make it a good image for visualization meditation to help develop concentration and awareness that can lead towards awakening and enlightenment.

a meditation on intention, action, result

As you have already read, actions consist of intention, action and result. If one or two elements are absent, then the karmic result is less; this applies both to skilful, positive actions and to unskilful, negative actions. In this context it is important to consider that all our actions are irrevocable. Once we have performed an action we cannot take it back – the karma has been created and we will definitely experience the effects in the future. Therefore it is important to think before we act, so that we can try to prevent ourselves acting out negative intentions and can lessen the intensity of the karma.

Although most of what happens to us is created by causes from the past, it is how we respond now that will create what comes into our karmic path in the future. So it is also important to think before we speak. Consider the impact of what you have to say on those who will hear you. Make sure that what you say is worthwhile, and that your words will spread harmony, not discord. For instance, when someone shouts at you, pause; you are under no obligation to shout back.

Reflect on the wisdom of thinking before you act in this meditation.

1 Sit comfortably with your back straight. Close your eyes and bring your attention to your breath. Observe your breathing for a few minutes to calm the mind.

2 Consider your usual behaviour, which is probably an automatic response to your feelings. You might think it is beneficial to act out your feelings immediately, but unreflective action can be destructive. This does not mean that spontaneity is unskilful, but it can take less than a second to check whether your action is skilful or not. Reflect upon the karmic impact of changing your behaviour in this manner, and resolve to try in future to think before doing.

3 Developing the art of listening to others helps you realize that you don't need to say everything that comes into your mind. Often in conversation with another person we are impatient to speak our thoughts, and can barely wait – not listening carefully, even sometimes with thinly veiled impatience – till they finish speaking. Yet conversing like this means we often say irrelevant things and have not given ourselves the best chance of learning something from the other person. Resolve in future to listen more attentively and patiently during conversations with others.

4 When someone is kind to us, we tend to be kind back; when someone is offensive, we are tempted to be rude to that person too. However, every time we respond to someone we are creating karma. Reflect on the importance of trying to be skilful in the way you respond to others by realizing that your actions will cause a karmic effect.

5 Return to watching your breath for a few minutes. Take a few quiet moments to reflect on your meditation before moving on with your daily life.

The Eight Auspicious Symbols: golden wheel, white conch shell, pair of golden fishes, victory banner, parasol, treasure vase, lotus and endless knot.

KARMA AND YOUR CAREER

Most people spend a large part of their life at work, so career choice is important for many reasons, such as job satisfaction, wages, holidays, working conditions and job security. For some people other – perhaps less obvious – issues are also important, and these are often concerned with values and ethics. Your own personal actions at work obviously create karma, but the complexity of karma indicates that the type of business your employer is involved in will also affect the karma of all employees. So even if you behave skilfully with wisdom and compassion at work, if your employer has an unethical business or corrupt business practices, then you too will create some collective negative karma.

Manjushri, the bodhisattva of wisdom, embodies the discriminating awareness of all the Buddhas. Bodhisattvas seek enlightenment for the benefit of all beings, not just the liberation of their own suffering. Manjushri is golden orange and sits in vajra posture, and his right hand wields a flaming sword of wisdom. His left hand, placed in front of his heart, holds the stem of a lotus that bears the Buddhist text Prajnaparamita, the Perfection of Wisdom.

what your job reveals about your karma

Your choice of career can reveal many things about the kind of person you are. For instance, those who work in a caring profession are probably concerned about the well-being of their clients and work colleagues, and are motivated to work in a role that allows them to be of benefit to others.

Conversely, those with few educational qualifications or little training usually end up in menial, basic jobs. Cleaning, waiting on tables, basic clerical work and so on are not jobs that enable the people doing them to express themselves creatively with ease, and offer few chances to reveal their abilities. However, in both examples we can see the influence of karma in the choice of job, even if this is not evident in the role itself.

Working as a teacher is a caring role that allows you to be of much benefit to others.

social influences

When people live or work together in some form of group they naturally influence each other. They are also affected by external influences, and most people simply go along with and unquestioningly follow the influences from their social environment. These influences start with the kind of family you are born into. If your family values educational achievement, and has the time and resources to ensure the children become well educated, then the children, once grown up, will have good job opportunities. On the other hand, if you are born into a poor family with low work expectations, then – even for intelligent or ambitious children – the chances of ending up with a good job are much less favourable. Your karmic imprints from past lives determined which kind of family you were born into in the first instance, and then the way in which you were educated and trained prepared you for your most likely work opportunities.

There are plenty of 'rags to riches' stories of people from poor or deprived backgrounds who did very well for themselves and ended up in powerful, wealthy careers, or of privileged people making a mess of their lives and falling off the career ladder. Nonetheless, the majority of people do fulfil the expectations that their background determines for them. For those who manage to change their predicted outcome, we can surmise that their personal karma had a stronger influence than their collective karma and their social environment. They succeeded, or failed, because some strong karmic imprint from past lives met the appropriate conditions in this lifetime and came to fruition.

the importance of good motivation

Your chosen job can also reveal things about the karma you create within your work. For instance, imagine your prime motivation is to make as much money as possible. Your career reflects this ambition, and your job may be stressful and target-driven to achieve high earnings. However, the ethical values of your profession, and whether your business is damaging to people or the environment, probably do not concern you. So, although you may become wealthy, you will also create negative karma, thereby causing yourself future suffering.

how to make your job more ethical

Trying to make your job more ethical might appear a difficult task. Surely as an employee your primary efforts must be to fulfil your allotted tasks, rather than trying to change the way the business works. An amusing story illustrates this dilemma.

A young, conscientious person worked as a waitress in a restaurant. As a vegetarian, she felt it was wrong to kill animals to eat, especially if they were killed in a non-humanitarian way. So whenever a customer requested lobster, she always told them lobster was off that night, even though there was a pail of live lobsters in the kitchen! As the customer would always order something else to eat, it is unlikely that she harmed the restaurant's profits, and she saved quite a few lobsters from the pot of boiling water that is their usual fate.

In most jobs you can find ways to improve working practice, such as encouraging recycling old papers.

practical suggestions

In most jobs you can find some ways (perhaps less dramatic than the one described above) to improve working practice. The list below suggests some simple ways to make your job more ethical:

- Ideally all your actions should arise from skilful mental qualities – intention – because then the karma of an altruistic action is more powerful. A seemingly kind action executed thoughtlessly can backfire and cause problems. For instance, rushing to help a colleague without enquiring whether they want assistance may cause them to feel angry, incompetent or helpless.

- Work colleagues may be difficult to get on with and you cannot be expected to like everyone at your job. However, you can be kind and courteous to everyone, even if you do not like some people.

- It is common not to respect the property of the company you work for, and many people are wasteful of paper and other materials. Try not to waste resources. Not only will your organization be grateful, but the environment will benefit from considerate use of natural resources and other work materials.

- Some people feel it is all right to take the odd bit of stationery or other work material home, although this still counts as stealing. Stealing is wrong and creates bad karma, even if it is from an organization, not a person. The argument that an organization expects its employees to steal a little bit does not make stealing ethical in any way.

- Only a few people really enjoy their job. Mostly our jobs are fundamentally a way to earn a living, even though we may feel some job satisfaction. There are moments during the working day when most of us feel lazy. At times like this it is easy to not do your work well, to let things slip, even if you know it might inconvenience someone further down the line. Although it is hard to stay motivated at times like these, making an extra effort to be conscientious maintains good working practice.

transforming bad working practices

Non-violent communication (or NVC) is a powerful method to help you transform bad working practices between work colleagues. Dealing skilfully with difficult work situations as they arise, through everyone involved undertaking a formal session of NVC, can prevent negative karma being created and generate a generally more pleasant working atmosphere. NVC is one of several different models of conflict resolution, but it is quick and easy to use in the workplace. It helps you to respond to others from a place of clarity and awareness, which facilitates true communication and develops respect for everyone's needs.

Non-violent communication aims to improve the connections between different people, initially by recognizing each individual's own, often repressed needs. This step is then followed by extending the recognition of each other's needs to reach out to all others in the situation. The four-step dialogue below can be used between two people or a group, whenever there is conflict in the workplace. You can offer it to your company as a quick, easy and practical ritual that respects the needs of everyone. The one golden rule is that each person speaks in turn for each of the four steps, and absolutely no interruptions are allowed. A clear, centred focus at all times is important for NVC to work effectively. This helps you transform your judgements about others by empathizing with their needs.

1 *Observations*: Firstly, observe what is actually happening in a conflict situation. Then try to articulate what you have observed without introducing any form of judgement or evaluation. Stick to what you see people doing, and acknowledge whether this is something you like or dislike – but don't judge the person for doing it.

2 *Feelings*: Secondly, after expressing your observations, express how you feel about what you observed (feelings are different from observations). Start each sentence with 'I feel ...'

3 *Needs*: Thirdly, express what your needs are in this situation. It is really important to connect with and open your heart, and to speak from this place with honesty. Remember that needs are universal, and others will express similar needs to yours, such as the need for clarity, honesty and respect and the need to feel safe.

4 *Requests*: Finally, request those changes that would enrich your working life, but without demanding anything. These requests must be for specific actions by the others involved, and they must be realistic and respectful. Make them with no expectation that the other person, or people, must comply. Start with 'I would like you to ...' – but be careful not to be demanding or unreasonable.

Throughout this four-step dialogue try to remain focused. Choose your language carefully, using words that promote trust and honesty, empathy and harmony. Avoid harsh, judgemental, angry and ambiguous words, as they will create negative karma.

Whenever problems arise between work colleagues, a formal session of NVC can help resolve the matter.

exploring the concept of right livelihood

Theravadan monastics live in dependence on alms provided by their lay supporters, and never even touch money.

Right Livelihood is one part of the Buddha's eight-step path towards awakening. The other seven steps are described in the last chapter of this book (see page 120), but we examine Right Livelihood here because it is appropriate to consider Buddha's guide to ethical working in the context of how your work affects your karma.

Right Livelihood is concerned with earning a living in an ethical manner. Traditionally it is based on the ancient Indian principle of ahimsa, or harmlessness, although to do your job successfully without harming anyone or anything has become much harder in the modern world since the time of the Buddha.

Monks and nuns, both Buddhist and Christian, traditionally do not work for money. In the Theravada Buddhist tradition, whose monks and nuns follow a similar lifestyle to the Buddha and his followers, monastics never even touch money. They live in dependence on alms provided by their lay supporters, who in turn are offered spiritual support and guidance by the monks and nuns. The monastics live simple lives of spiritual practice and are worthy of support, so in this context they represent the pinnacle of Right Livelihood. However, many of us do need to earn a living, and it can be hard to find an ethical career.

profits or ethics?

Businesses in the modern world – especially in the wealthy developed countries of the West – are often more interested in maximizing profits than in being ethical, so many contemporary jobs do not fulfil the principle of harmlessness. For instance, insurance companies spend a lot of time attempting to invalidate people's claims so that they only have to pay out in as few cases as possible. This, of course, causes much suffering (and sometimes harm) to those people who believed they had a valid claim, but who do not receive payment. It also creates bad karma, especially for the bosses and owners of the company, but to a lesser extent also for the employees.

However, insurance companies seem mild in the bad karma they create compared to arms dealers, who are responsible for so much death, destruction and suffering. Buddha indicated that any job that causes harm should be avoided, so it is important to consider what the company you work for actually does. Any business that causes harm to people, animals or the environment is best avoided, even if you work in a minor role, such as a secretary or driver.

choosing a good career

In order to not only avoid causing bad karma, but also try and actively create good karma, you can choose a career that helps people, such as becoming a doctor, nurse or social worker, or working for a human-rights organization or environmental protection agency. Such work actively responds to the suffering of others and is of great benefit to them. However, not everyone is suited to such demanding roles, and as long as you check that the business you work in is not harmful, then your job itself is not creating bad karma.

You might wonder why your job is so important in terms of creating good or bad karma. We have already considered earlier in this chapter how much time is spent at work, but work is also an activity and involves numerous actions during the working day – many more so than resting quietly at home. The potential for creating karma is therefore much greater. Buddha taught another useful criteria for work that it is beneficial to consider: that your wages should be earnt according to certain standards. These are that your job must be legal, non-violent and honest, and should not cause harm to others.

ethical investment

A very few individuals are so wealthy that they do not need to work, but use their capital to generate an income instead. For these lucky people, they need to consider how their money is invested to avoid causing bad karma. So, in the same way that most of us consider how we can earn money in an ethical way, they must check that they don't own shares in companies that cause harm, such as tobacco companies or those that produce toxic waste. By investing in ethical business ventures that actively try to be of benefit to others, they can create good karma.

It can be a useful exercise to consider all the criteria listed above for Right Livelihood in relation to your own job. If you find that you are dissatisfied with your job, feel trapped in an unsuitable role or discover that your work is not as ethical as you had assumed, you can use the principles of Right Livelihood to assess the current situation. These principles can then help you decide how to move on, and what alternative career or type of work you would like to do.

gap-year opportunities

Many young people take a now-fashionable gap year, either before or after university. This offers them the opportunity to combine travel with volunteer work in Developing World countries. These young people can choose to work protecting endangered animals, teaching children or adults or helping with scientific projects. All these gap-year activities teach a valuable lesson: that it is worthwhile helping those less fortunate than yourself. On their return, such young people are more likely to choose ethical jobs and continue their good work.

By now it should be clear that making large amounts of money is not the only criterion for work. Even though modern society has elevated material well-being above social responsibility and personal conscience, you can never find true happiness if your job is unethical or causes suffering. Taking a possibly low paid job that offers you the chance to be of benefit to others will give you greater job satisfaction and create good karma.

Volunteer work in the Developing World before going to university is a good way of helping those less fortunate than yourself.

how to find a new, more ethical career

Reading through this chapter may have left you with some questions about whether or not you are in the right job. Feelings of confusion and doubt about what you really want to do with your life may also have arisen.

Using the short questionnaire below can help you resolve your feelings about your current work situation, and can aid you in discovering what kind of work you might prefer to do. You may find some old, unresolved issues coming to mind. Alternatively, you may find that you don't want (or feel the need) to make any dramatic changes in your work. Either way, this is an interesting exercise to explore your feelings about your career.

questionnaire

Be scrupulously honest in your answers – only you need see this questionnaire and your responses. Sometimes your answers to questionnaires show how you would like to be, rather than how you actually are.

- Is your job ethical? If not, do you feel strongly enough about this to want to change jobs? These are two important and interconnected questions. If you decide your job is not as ethical as you would like, then you must work out whether this really bothers you. If your feelings are mild, then changing your job solely on this basis could make you feel resentful. You might have to give up a lot that you like, such as good wages and holidays. If you reach this conclusion, it is better to make less radical changes. Look again at the suggestions earlier in the chapter (see page 55) and see if there are minor alterations you can make within your current job to improve the ethics. Alternatively, if you feel strongly about working for an unethical business, you should explore all the options to change your job.

- What is the nature of your job? Would you prefer to work in a more caring role? Although your current job may appear neutral from a karmic perspective and may not cause you to create bad karma, you may feel you would like to be of greater benefit to others or the environment and thereby intentionally create good karma. If so, explore the possibility of changing your current career, perhaps to one of the caring professions.

- Are you happy in your job? As you have already read, happiness is more important than money. Of course it is important to earn an adequate living, but if you are unhappy in your work, you are more likely to act negatively and create bad karma, even if this is unintentional. If you are not happy, explore what kind of work would make you feel more contented.

how to do cobra pose

Bhujanga means serpent or snake, and Bhujangasana (or cobra pose) is a back bend, which promotes flexibility and strength in the spine and encourages the chest to open. Do not do cobra pose if you have a back problem or are pregnant.

1 Lie stretched out on the floor, facing down. Place your hands under your shoulders and press the tops of your feet, thighs and pubis firmly into the floor. On an inhalation, lift your chest and arms off the floor. Breathe out and place your hands back on the floor.

2 On the next inhalation straighten your arms to raise your chest up again. Ensure you distribute the back bend evenly throughout your entire spine. Hold the pose for 15–30 seconds, breathing easily. Release back to the floor with an exhalation.

KARMA AND PROSPERITY

When we look at the world it seems so unfair in terms of how wealth is shared out: a few people have much more than they could ever need, while many others do not have enough for even their most basic living requirements. Despite concerted national and international efforts to redress this long-term, ongoing situation, not much changes and the solutions of politics and economics are clearly limited. Such endemic inequality indicates that karma and prosperity are intimately interlinked. In this thought-provoking chapter you can explore wealth, poverty, karma and the intricate web of relationships between them.

Vajradhara, the Primordial Buddha, seated in vajra posture and holding a vajra and bell, symbols of compassion and wisdom.

why some people have wealth and others do not

From the perspective of karma, the simple answer to the conundrum of the unfair distribution of wealth is that wealth is the karmic fruit of generosity, whereas poverty is the karmic result of avarice.

Although this statement is true, there are other factors involved in why some people have wealth and others do not, such as where you were born and what job you do. However, it is the link between karma and prosperity that concerns us here. If you wish to create the karma to be wealthy in a future life, then it is important to practise generosity in this life and to examine your attitudes to giving. Your motivation should include the wish to benefit others with your wealth, once you acquire it – otherwise the selfish desire for wealth to benefit only yourself will create negative karma.

A great Buddhist teacher said that practising generosity causes roots of goodness to sprout in this life and the next.

the spirit of giving

The major karmic contribution to your own current and future prosperity is being generous to others. Generosity includes an attitude of mind as much as the giving of material objects, time, energy and attention. In Buddhism generosity is called dana, and means giving or charity. More specifically, dana is the spirit of generosity together with actual acts of giving. Generosity is therefore intimately linked with karma, because acts of generosity are skilful and positive and cause good karma. On the other hand, neglecting to give when you have the opportunity and means to do so is mean-spirited, unskilful behaviour that creates bad karma.

Generosity is a powerful antidote to attachment and greed. By taking every opportunity that arises to practise generosity, you will gradually begin to develop a giving mind. Transforming attachment into generosity purifies negative karma and creates positive karma. It is not the value of what you give that is important. A great Buddhist teacher once said that to give even a single coin, or a single blade of grass, causes roots of goodness in this life and other lives to sprout. This statement shows that it is the intention of generosity that is the essence of giving. The traditional Buddhist tale outlined below is a lovely story of true generosity.

a tale of generosity

Two brothers shared the family farm, and one of them was married with a family while the other was single. The single man thought often of his brother, and of how with his wife and children he would need more than his half of the farm proceeds. Secretly at night he would go to the barn and move a few sacks of his own grain to his brother's side. The married man thought often how his brother must be lonely, and that if he had a little extra money perhaps he might find a wife and settle down. He too secretly moved a few sacks of his grain to his brother's side from time to time. Neither brother could ever work out why he had so much grain, yet both felt blessed and happy.

a meditation on using wealth to generate good karma

Being generous to others is an important practice for generating good karma, but, frequently, giving is not done with a pure attitude, so the resulting karma is mixed. The following meditation helps you examine the motivations and intentions that lie behind different types of giving, so that you can learn how to give in the most generous way that generates only good karma.

1 Sit comfortably with your back straight. Close your eyes and bring your attention to your breath. Observe your breathing for a few minutes to calm the mind.

2 Buddha described three types of generosity: the beggarly kind, the friendly kind and the princely kind. In this meditation you will reflect upon the three kinds of giving and the different karma they generate.

3 *Beggarly generosity*: This is giving away things you don't want – items that are cluttering up your home or gifts you have been given that you don't care for. Although better than giving nothing, such actions are not real generosity. You should not feel you are being especially generous, because you are not affecting your own desires and needs, nor are you challenging your attachment to any of the things you give. In fact, beggarly giving may just be a way of tidying up your home, and the resulting karma is not very positive.

4 *Friendly generosity*: This is when you freely share what you have with others, and is better than the beggarly kind. However, with friendly giving you need to check your intention carefully. Consider that you invite a friend to eat dinner with you at a restaurant at your expense, which seems a generous action. However, perhaps the restaurant you choose serves the kind of food you yourself enjoy eating. Perhaps you expect your friend to offer to contribute to the meal and are displeased if they don't. Or you expect an invitation, or gratitude, in return and are disappointed if this doesn't happen. Check whether you practise friendly giving purely, or whether you are pleasing yourself or have expectations of gratitude or reciprocation. Because friendly giving is usually confused, as described here, the karmic result is mixed.

5 *Princely generosity*: This is when you give away more than you keep, with no expectation of return. It is giving in order to give; the other forms are giving in order to get. Princely giving is quite difficult to practise purely. Try to remember an instance when you practised princely giving, then check your motivation carefully. Was there any expectation of a return – even if this was only of gratitude? Even the motivation to generate good karma, or giving because you think you ought to, is a little tainted. The aim in princely giving is to give purely out of compassion, and this creates good karma.

Four-armed Avalokiteshvara, the white bodhisattva of compassion. His arms represent the generosity of love, compassion, joy and equanimity.

karmic reflections on poverty

The karmic reflections below are designed to help you think openly and creatively about the connections between karma and poverty, wealth and generosity. Reading them will stimulate thoughtful enquiry in a similar way to the meditation on pages 68–9.

how to do warrior pose

Virabhadrasana is the spiritual warrior who bravely battles the universal enemy of ignorance, the ultimate source of all suffering. Thewarrior pose is also to do with abundance and the spirit of generosity.

1 Stand with your feet wide apart, turn your right leg out 90 degrees and swing your hips to face your right leg. Inhale and, as you exhale, bend your right knee.

2 As you inhale, raise your arms above your head. Bring your palms together and hold for 30–60 seconds. Repeat on the other side.

food for thought

Try choosing one reflection that especially piques your curiosity and spend a few minutes of your time contemplating its meaning.

- Being generous to those in need, through acts of secret or anonymous giving, ensures that your motivation is not to receive praise and gratitude, or something in return.

- It is easy to give with an unwholesome attitude. When a beggar asks you for money, examine your reaction. Most people turn away and choose not to give at all; this can be appropriate if you don't have any spare change, or feel certain the person is not genuine. Nonetheless the beggar is a human being with feelings and needs, and even if you choose not to give, you can be polite and not cause the person to feel badly. If you decide to give, do so with kindness; words of encouragement or a smile can make the beggar feel just as happy as a few coins.

- Giving skilfully creates more positive karma than giving resentfully, or not at all.

- You have no way of knowing if you yourself might end up in poverty. Wealth can easily be lost. Imagine yourself poor and destitute, and reflect on how you would wish others to offer you kindness and generosity.

- No one who has been generous has ever perished in destitution.

- Only give material benefit to those in need as you can afford to. Generosity must be realistic to be skilful. If you give so much that you cannot look after yourself and end up destitute, this does not cause good karma for yourself, and only creates problems for those who must look after you.

- Even if you cannot afford to give material help to those in need, thinking about them with kindness and compassion, rather than scorn or blame, develops the mind and spirit of generosity.

- True generosity in response to poverty is when you consider the other person's needs as being higher than your own, and give in this spirit.

- Those who are poor, but have enough to meet their basic needs, can be happy, because happiness does not depend on wealth. However, those in dire poverty who cannot afford food, clean water and shelter can only suffer.

- Giving too much of yourself to others in your personal life, or through the caring professions, can lead to exhaustion. Then you can no longer work for the benefit of others and cease to create positive karma. You must take adequate care of yourself to be able to keep giving out energy and goodwill to others.

a ritual to attract abundance

The following simple little ritual is drawn from the Western magical tradition. Authentic magic has an inherent understanding of the law of karma, because the energy of magic works in harmony with all universal energies and laws. So, from the perspective of magic as well as karma, generosity plays a significant role in attracting abundance.

It is important to realize that attracting abundance is not just about increasing wealth; abundance also refers to developing all creative endeavours and spiritual growth. Abundance rituals are best undertaken during the spring and when the moon is waxing and nearly full. The plentiful, lush new growth of spring and the round fullness of the moon both reveal Nature in an expansive mood.

Important objects for use in abundance rituals are anything green, silver coins, sprouting plants and rich natural scents, such as essential oils. In keeping with the principle of trying to create good karma, this ritual should be undertaken with the prime motivation of benefiting another, and benefiting yourself should only be a secondary motivation. The ritual is fundamentally about generosity, although it also incorporates the universal principle of 'like producing like' – in other words, your generosity to others may bring an act of generosity back to you.

1 Think of a friend (someone with whom you have a karmic connection) who is in real need of extra money, perhaps for something essential that they cannot afford. Spend a few minutes reflecting on the kindness and affection your friend shows to you, and think fondly of that person.

2 Take a single banknote: a low-denomination one if you are not feeling wealthy or a high-value note if you can afford it. Consider that the money has no inherent value – it is just a piece of paper – and that money itself is neither good nor bad; it is the way money is used that determines whether the outcome is positive or negative.

3 Take a candle and rub over it a few drops of a rich scented essential oil, such as patchouli, rose, jasmine, cinnamon, ginger or sandalwood. It is important that you like the fragrance. Light the candle and spend a few minutes enjoying the vaporized fragrance of the essential oil.

4 Wrap the banknote in a plain piece of green paper, without anything that could identify you, then seal it inside an envelope and address it to your friend.

5 Place the sealed envelope near the candle (but not so close that it might catch fire!) and spend a few minutes meditating on generosity.

6 Post the envelope to your friend on the twelfth day of the month. This act of generosity will create good karma, but the magical ritual may also bring you an act of generosity from someone else.

Abundance rituals are best performed during the lush new growth of Spring when Nature is in an expansive mood.

KARMA AND RELATIONSHIPS

Love is perhaps the most powerful human emotion we can ever experience. We express love through the different relationships we have with the other people in our lives, and we love our parents, siblings, children, lovers and friends in very different ways. Love can be unskilful and destructive as well as skilful and fulfilling, so there is enormous potential to create both good and bad karma in our relationships. In this chapter we look at our relationships with others, how to make them truly loving and how to avoid being trapped in a negative, shadow expression of love.

Green Tara, the mother of all the Buddhas, is the female bodhisattva of compassion and mercy. Also known as the saviouress, she protects all beings from the Eight Great Fears, or mental defilements. Her green colour represents the air element, and symbolizes the perfect ability of her compassionate activities in all directions simultaneously.

living in the world skilfully with others

Everyone needs friendship and love, and we share our world with many other people. Living your life with an open mind, a warm heart and kind feelings towards everyone creates the karma for you to experience love and happiness yourself.

However, developing a loving attitude towards those you feel indifferent to or dislike is difficult. For instance, when people are kind to you, it is easy to feel loving towards them, but when someone is unkind, it is hard to feel any affection in return. Nonetheless, cultivating a loving response to others at all times – whatever their attitude towards you – creates the karma for you to receive love and happiness in the future.

the nature of friendship

Contemplating the nature of friendship can make it easier to cherish all the people in your life. For instance, think about your best friend. There was a time in your life when this person was unknown to you, and you had no idea a friendship between the two of you would develop. Perhaps you had a dear friend earlier in life who moved away, or with whom you fell out. You might have an old girlfriend or boyfriend whom you once loved very much, but who now means nothing to you. These cases show that friends can become enemies; people to whom you are indifferent can become friends; and lovers can become strangers. The Buddha taught that because relationships change over time, it is advisable to cherish everyone you meet as a dear friend to avoid creating negative karmic relationships.

The Buddhist teachings explain how karma operates over many different lifetimes. To clarify this point the teachings encourage us to reflect on the idea that all beings have, in one lifetime or another, been our mother. Because everyone you meet has at one time during your many lifetimes been your mother and taken loving care of you, an appropriate response is to feel love for all these people. This doesn't mean you should become sentimental or overly emotional, but when you encounter someone who is making life difficult or unpleasant for you, if you remember that previously this person was once your loving mother, it is easier not to respond badly to their current negative behaviour.

open your heart

Our different relationships bring with them diverse joys and challenges. Although we relate differently to family and friends, lovers and work colleagues, the essence of all relationships is an opening of the heart and mind to each other. Opening your heart fully to another can feel risky, but it enables you to be more aware and appreciative of that person, and can lead to total acceptance of them. You then love that person unconditionally – both for their good qualities and their eccentricities – and appreciate them for who they are.

how to do child pose

Balasana, or child pose, is a nurturing posture resembling the baby in the womb. The pose soothes, calms and develops flexibility and softness.

Kneel with your ankles and knees close together and, as you inhale, lift your arms above your head. As you exhale, sit back on your heels, then fold your body forward until your forehead rests on the floor. Place your hands alongside your feet, relax and focus on the breath. Hold for a few minutes.

a meditation on equanimity with others

Although you may not like or feel a connection with everyone you meet, you can at least try to be kind and courteous to those people you don't instinctively like, as you would wish them to be kind and courteous to you. You can reflect that these people are also looking for happiness and trying to avoid suffering, just like you.

In this way, although you still may not like them, it is easier to act pleasantly towards them and not create any negative karma. As long as you actively discriminate between those you love, those you hate and those to whom you feel indifferent, you will not really understand what love is. True love is not preferential.

Meditating on equanimity in a temple with others is a reminder of how all people are equal inside a place of worship.

1 Sit comfortably with your back straight. Close your eyes and bring your attention to your breath. Observe your breathing for a few minutes to calm the mind.

2 Visualize three people sitting or standing in front of you. One is your dear friend, for whom you feel much affection. The second is your enemy, someone you dislike strongly. The third is a stranger, towards whom you feel indifferent. Observe how your feelings differ towards these three people.

3 Focus on your friend. Notice how you feel warmth and affection towards your friend, because this person is consistently kind to you.

4 Bring your attention to your enemy. Observe the sadness or anger you feel because this person has hurt or annoyed you.

5 Think of the stranger. Your feelings towards the stranger are probably less intense than your affection for your friend and your dislike for your enemy. You feel indifferent to this person.

6 Recognize that how you feel about these three people is based solely on what they do for you. Imagine that your friend suddenly turned against you. Your feelings of affection might turn to hostility. Realize that your affection was based on how this person could be of benefit to you, rather than on their inherent qualities.

7 Reflect on what might happen if your enemy offered you some kindness or assistance. You might feel that you had misjudged this person. If they were repeatedly kind to you, your hostility might eventually turn to affection.

8 The same is true about your indifference towards the stranger. Imagine that you meet, have a conversation and realize you have a lot in common, and that feelings of friendship arise.

9 Reflect on the fragility of all human relationships and how easily they can change. There is no logical reason why you should have feelings of affection, dislike and indifference towards other people. Your friend was a stranger before you met; your enemy might have been a friend with whom you fell out; and the stranger could easily become a friend.

10 Resolve to have respect and concern for everyone. Relationships change, and developing equanimity for all is a wise response to our impermanent world.

learning to let go

A great Buddhist teacher had a beautiful vase in his room. Everyone who visited him admired this exquisite vase. One day a student came to see him and opened the door clumsily. The vase fell to the floor and smashed to pieces.

The horrified student started to apologize, but noticed that her teacher was smiling and didn't seem upset that his beautiful vase was broken. The student asked her teacher why he didn't mind losing his precious vase. The teacher replied, 'I always told myself the vase was already broken, so when one day it inevitably broke, I would not feel its loss. You too can learn to let go of your attachments in this way.'

change causes dissatisfaction

This story shows that impermanence and change are part of existence, even though we often find this fact disagreeable and are attached to the objects and people in our lives. Yet impermanence is easily visible all around: the orange rotting in the fruit bowl over a few days, the wilted roses that were bought fresh last week. Change continually permeates our existence, causing suffering and dissatisfaction. For instance, imagine on a hot sunny day you are enjoying lying in the sun, but after a while you become too hot and find relief by jumping into a cool swimming pool and splashing around. However, after some time you feel cold and tired, and need to change things again by getting out of the pool and lying in the sun.

All material things are inherently impermanent because they come into being dependent on conditions. For instance, the existence of a table depends on the tree that supplied the wood and on the carpenter who fashioned it. Such phenomena are temporal, existing in a moment in time; but however short or long, eventually the conditions that brought about their existence will change, and the object will cease to be. Life itself is impermanent and will transform into death one day. There is something deeply poignant about impermanence, and contemplating the brevity of existence encourages us to value our own lives and everyone in them.

everything will end

All things – including relationships – will change and eventually end, because it is their nature to do so. Realizing that everything is impermanent is crucial to understanding karma. Once you know that all things are impermanent, it becomes easier to be less attached to your relationships. Your desire for your beloved then becomes less obsessive, true love blossoms and you generate less negative karma through attachment.

Most relationships are challenging in some way, and even a blissfully happy relationship will have its ups and downs. All relationships will finally end with partners breaking up, or with the death of one or both people involved. Learning to let go of attachment to your relationships and friendships, by understanding impermanence and change, helps avoid causing negative karma.

Watching fruit deteriorate over a few days offers a powerful image of the transient nature of all things.

a visualization on letting go

A tightly closed fist tries to grasp hold of things, but they slip away because of the grasping, just as if you try to hold on to running water, it slips through your hands. Opening to life as it unfolds is like letting a stream wash over your open hands, and means that you can appreciate life as it happens. Then you can let it go naturally as it flows by, without trying to hold it back.

From the perspective of many lifetimes, trying to hold on to anything or anyone is pointless. All relationships arise and pass, so let them go easily when their time is up. If you practise letting go as much as possible throughout your lifetime, not only do you create positive karma for a better rebirth, but at death you will be able to let go of life itself a little easier. This visualization on letting go is especially helpful if you have recently lost someone dear to you through death or the break-up of a relationship.

1 Sit comfortably with your back straight. Close your eyes and bring your attention to your breath. Observe your breathing for a few minutes to calm the mind.

2 The intention of this visualization is to honour the person with whom you had a relationship and who has died or moved on. Spend a few minutes meditating on impermanence – that all things will pass – and resolve to let this person go in peace and love, without attachment.

3 Bring the person to mind and recall shared moments together. Spend a few minutes recollecting different special times you enjoyed together, and recall the love and affection you felt for each other. Although the relationship is over, the love you experienced remains in your heart. Think of the person fondly, and thank him or her for sharing time with you.

4 See the person with you, enclosed in a circle of gold or white light. Visualize a farewell ceremony between the two of you: a simple kiss or hug goodbye might feel right, or perhaps some personal ritual that held significance for you both.

5 When it feels the right time to let go, visualize the circle dividing like a fertilized ovum, separating the two of you. The two circles of light spin away from each other slowly into the vastness of space and time in the universe.

6 Sit quietly with your thoughts and feelings as you visualize the other person's circle of light slowly moving away. Realize the pointlessness and foolishness of attachment – how such feelings cannot change the situation, but will only create negative karma.

7 When you feel ready to move on, reflect that this visualization has honoured both of you and enabled you to let go with grace, love and dignity. Wish the person well and let them go.

Water flowing over your hands is a symbol of opening to life as it unfolds without trying to hold on to anything.

major relationships

Many of the people with whom you have a major relationship in this current life you will also have had a relationship with in previous lives. As already mentioned, relationships have immense potential to create karma, both positive and negative.

These karmic relationships will change over different lifetimes – for instance, your current husband may have been your daughter in a previous life – but the karmic bond is strong enough to ensure that you have another significant relationship. These meetings over many lifetimes are not a sentimental way of love enduring beyond the grave, as is sometimes depicted in films and novels. Each lifetime that you have a major relationship with someone – whether this is your mother, lover, enemy or other significant person in your life – offers an opportunity to purify the negative karma between you. In other words, you have been given the chance to get things right this time around.

the power of attachment and desire

Of course the reverse is also true to some extent, and any positive karma created between two people in a relationship during one lifetime may well create the cause for them to meet and have a genuine, loving relationship in a future life. However, because attachment and desire are such powerful impulses in major relationships, encountering each other again is usually about learning something new together and purifying past mistakes.

Although you might feel this is rather a conjectural theory, many of us on first meeting another person occasionally have a curious feeling of having met them before – a sense of déjà vu. Such feelings are clearly not proof of any kind, but they do indicate strongly some kind of previous karmic relationship. Whenever this feeling of knowing each other already occurs (although this may not have been possible in this life), there is a good chance these two people may form a major relationship of some kind.

parents and children

The bond between parents and children is especially powerful, and often has different phases, ranging from unconditional love to great difficulty – particularly when it is time for the child to mature and become his or her own person. It can be helpful for both parents and children to regard problems in the relationship as a karmic opportunity to try and truly express love for each other in the face of difficulty. Problems can be understood as a chance to purify previous negative karma, and embraced as a way of progressing spiritually.

Soulmates and lovers face different challenges, and sexuality comes into play. Powerful physical urges are accompanied by strong emotional needs, and attachment to your lover can cause jealousy and the possibility of unskilful behaviour. If you give your lover space to be who he or she is, as well as being with you, then both people and their relationship can flourish.

The powerful bond between mother and baby may well be the karmic result of a relationship in a previous life.

the difference between love and attachment

It is easy to confuse love and attachment. When you truly love someone, you want them to be happy, whether or not their happiness depends on being with you. Being attached to someone is not a full or complete expression of love.

Attachment demands that another person love you in return for you loving them. In this way, you try to make someone else responsible for your happiness, rather than accepting responsibility for your own happiness. The clinging nature of attachment is unwholesome and can easily lead to the creation of negative karma.

questionnaire

The questions below, when answered honestly, will help you tell the difference between love and attachment, and can assist you in developing truly loving relationships.

• Sexual love is a special form of love that you share with another person. Being in love with someone and expressing love sexually can make you feel vulnerable, so you need to be especially careful that you behave in a way that will contribute to both people's happiness. Ask yourself: Is my partner's happiness as important to me as my own? If not, then your love is tainted with attachment and you run the risk of acting in a way that will create negative karma.

• When you first feel sexual attraction to someone, it is easy to assume that you have fallen in love. Ask yourself: Is this person someone with whom I can develop a lasting, loving relationship? If not, you are confusing attachment to sexual desire with love. If you have sex before establishing a loving, respectful relationship – hoping that sex will lead to love – you may end up feeling hurt and rejected.

• When you feel a strong physical attraction to someone, ask yourself: Can I look beyond this person's superficial appearance that has caused my desire, and open my heart to love the whole person? It is easy to become attached to appearances, but remember that beauty soon fades, while true love endures.

• When you fall in love, you create an ideal fiction about your new friend, who seems wonderful in every way. However, after some time you may start to notice faults in your friend, and realize that he or she is not as perfect as you first thought.

Ask yourself: Can I let go of my attachment to the fiction of perfection in my new lover? Being realistic at the beginning of a relationship helps love to develop and avoids disappointment later on.

• There is a familiar saying: 'If you really love someone, let them go.' This expresses well the nature of attachment that causes insecure, clinging behaviour. Ask yourself: Do I give my lover adequate space to be himself or herself, or do I always try to be with him or her? True love is spacious and trusting, while attachment is claustrophobic and distrustful.

how to do assisted tailor pose

Baddha konasana, or assisted tailor pose, is a lovely posture to do with a partner, perhaps while you meditate on the difference between true love and attachment.

Sit back-to-back, cross-legged, making sure you are both supporting each other fully. Tune into your partner's breathing and let your breathing rhythms harmonize. Reflect that a loving relationship relies on mutual support.

the difference between healthy and unhealthy relationships

The essence of all healthy relationships is respect, which manifests as gratitude that you can spend time with each other, enjoying each other's company.

However, it is all too easy to take people for granted, to forget that they contribute towards your happiness and well-being through their unselfish kindness and affection. You begin wanting to see them only because they fulfil your needs emotionally and, with lovers, physically. You forget what you can do for them. Taking others for granted in this way is a major characteristic of unhealthy relationships.

A simple example of common everyday behaviour shows clearly the difference between healthy and unhealthy relationships. If someone you care for looks at you with a kind, affectionate smile, it makes you feel happy. Conversely, if this person scowls at you angrily, you feel uncomfortable and upset. So from your own experience you can see that everyone wants to feel kindness and affection from others, and does not want to experience their negativity.

opening up to others

Relationships include minor and temporary relationships, as well as the major associations with the important people in your life. Developing the habit of being kind and loving towards all the people you encounter creates the karma to find love and happiness yourself. With healthy relationships you continually try to be caring and affectionate to others, and this helps you move away from narrow self-centredness and open up to other people. Such an attitude is humbling and shows the foolishness of the selfish arrogance that is typical in unhealthy relationships; you feel gratitude for your own existence and for all these other people with whom you have relationships, and without whom you would be alone.

By cultivating genuine affection for others in your heart, you can spread a little happiness to all the people in your life; and when people are happy, their hearts open and they tend to respond more lovingly to others. So approaching others with warm affection means they are likely to react in a caring, friendly manner towards you. This mutual exchange of affection helps to foster a generally happy environment, and creates the karmic cause to experience happiness in the future.

projections and idealization

In unhealthy relationships there is a tendency to project your fantasies onto those you love, and then you end up with unrealistic expectations of them. When your loved one fails to live up to your idealized image of him or her, tensions arise and cause difficulties between you. You have to learn how to move beyond the illusions you have created about that person, and get to know them fully. Try to accept them for who they are and to appreciate the whole person – their faults as well as what you like about them. In healthy relationships you recognize and value people for who they really are, beyond your projections and fantasies about them.

how to do forward bend pose

This adaptation of a yoga posture shows how relationships can be mutually supportive.

Sit on the floor, with your legs outstretched and feet together, and with your partner sitting in front of you. Rest your feet on the front of your partner's ankles and take hold of his or her hands. Your partner then gently lifts and stretches your arms, moving them forwards and upwards, while ensuring that you are not straining yourself.

a meditation on loving kindness

In Buddhism, the Pali word metta means 'loving kindness'. This frequently practised Buddhist meditation cultivates spaciousness of mind and openness of heart.

Loving kindness is the genuine feeling of concern for the happiness and well-being of others. However, we must first develop loving kindness towards ourselves, because sometimes we feel we don't deserve to be happy, or we judge ourselves harshly. Loving and accepting ourselves is the first step towards developing loving kindness towards others.

1 Sit comfortably with your back straight. Close your eyes and bring your attention to your breath. Observe your breathing for a few minutes to calm the mind. Alongside watching the breath, try to discover within your heart a warm, caring feeling towards all life.

2 Start to develop loving kindness towards yourself. Accept yourself as someone with faults and good qualities, but who also has the right to try to find happiness and avoid suffering. Perhaps sometimes you feel you don't deserve to be happy, or you judge yourself unkindly. Soften these harsh feelings and feel compassion for this suffering being.

3 Silently say to yourself, 'May I live in safety. May I experience happiness, peace and good health. May my daily life go easily, without problems.' Repeat these phrases silently several times and reflect on their meaning. Try to cultivate your feelings rather than your intellect.

4 After a few minutes bring to mind someone who has helped you, such as a benefactor, teacher, parent or partner. Choose someone for whom you feel great respect, love and gratitude. Repeat the phrases above, using that person's name. Remember his or her great kindness towards you, and feel loving kindness towards this person.

5 After a few minutes include a good friend, someone for whom you feel real affection, and repeat the phrases using their name. Then include someone towards whom you have no strong feelings. This is harder, so remind yourself that this person has the same right as you to find freedom from suffering and discover happiness. Generate a feeling of loving kindness towards this person.

6 Now include an enemy, someone who has harmed you. You don't have to like the person, or condone their negative behaviour, but you can develop loving kindness towards them and not wish them harm. Often people who behave badly experience much suffering, so offering them loving kindness might help them behave more considerately. Reflect that sometimes you too behave badly. Generate loving kindness towards this person.

7 Finally include all beings everywhere, and radiate feelings of loving kindness towards them. Reflect that we are all interdependent with each other; no one lives in isolation. Rest in the warm feeling of all-pervasive loving kindness for as long as you wish. Dedicate the merit from this meditation towards the happiness of all beings everywhere.

Kuan Yin ('she who listens to the laments of the world'), the bodhisattava of mercy and compassion.

a bonding ritual for couples

Of all the important relationships in life, the most intimate and passionate is with your sexual partner. The deep level of intimacy created through making love physically with the person you cherish creates a unique bond between the two of you that is private and special; no one else can share in your unique experience. However, the intensity of feelings underlying the deep love you have for each other can also create problems.

The bonding ritual below is a creative, mutually respectful way of expressing sensitivity and consideration for each other, which can deepen the bond between you and help resolve any difficult issues.

1 Start off with both you and your partner sitting comfortably facing each other, either on floor cushions or on chairs, whichever is more comfortable and appropriate to enable you to do the ritual. Sit so that you are close enough to each other to be able to hold hands, if you choose. Set a quiet alarm to ring in five minutes or so.

2 Both of you should close your eyes, rest your hands on your own knees and bring your attention to your breath. Observe your breathing for a few minutes to calm the mind. Be aware of your partner's closeness and the sensation of their breathing nearby.

3 Open your eyes when you hear the alarm bell ring. You may now hold hands, if you choose, or leave them resting comfortably on your knees.

4 Reflect on the importance of taking time to get know each other in a different way from your normal life together. Gaze into your partner's eyes and appreciate the warmth and love that you see reflected back at you. You might feel like laughing because you are uncomfortable or embarrassed, and this is fine to begin with, but try to let these feelings pass. Trust your partner and yourself in this expression of love.

5 Experience the deep karmic connection between you. You will feel this in your heart, but explore the feeling – see if you also experience it in other places in your body. Stay with the physical sensations and really feel what they are like.

6 Now speak some words of love and appreciation to your partner. Tell them how much you love and care for them, how much you appreciate them taking care of you. Try to be spontaneous and creative; the old clichés of love can be meaningful, but creating your own special way of telling your partner about your love can be deeply moving.

7 Return to silence and gazing into each other's eyes for a few minutes. Now each of you should recite in turn a poem or piece of prose that really speaks of your love for each other.

8 Finally close your eyes, return your hands to your knees if you have been holding hands and spend a few minutes meditating together silently.

HEALING KARMIC SUFFERING

The negative karma you have accrued over your many different lifetimes will manifest — in one lifetime or another — as suffering of some kind. Minor bad karma causes mild suffering to mature, while major karmic transgressions bring to fruition much greater suffering. However, most people don't live solely lives of suffering; they experience good times as well as bad, which reflects the balance of positive and negative karma they have created, which has met appropriate conditions and come to fruition in this lifetime. This mix of good and bad karma also indicates that the karmic potential of negative actions — suffering — can be transformed and healed through some form of purification.

Avalokiteshvara (or Chenrezig in Tibetan) is the bodhisattva of compassion and the patron deity of Tibet. The Dalai Lama is said to be a reincarnation of Chenrezig. Avalokiteshvara holds the Wish-Fulfilling Jewel before his heart with his two lower hands, and a crystal rosary and a lotus in his upper right and left hands. His four arms symbolize the 'four immeasurables' of compassion, love, sympathetic joy and equanimity.

transforming karmic suffering

Throughout this life and many previous lives we have all accumulated a great deal of bad karma, some of which will cause an unpleasant effect in this life, and the remainder will condition our future lives adversely.

This troubling prognosis prompts the question: Is there anything you can do about all the negative karma you have created over your many different lifetimes? Obviously it would be preferable not to experience all the karmic results! Fortunately there is a tried-and-trusted way in which you can clear your negative karma. This is purification, which offers you the opportunity to transform at least some of your bad karma in this life, here and now.

Essentially, purification first of all requires you to understand that you have behaved badly on some occasions and in certain situations. Then you must accept and take full responsibility for your unskilful behaviour. This stage can be quite difficult because it is tempting to blame others for making you behave badly, although ultimately only you are responsible for your own behaviour. The next stage is that you must sincerely regret and repent your negative actions, and promise to try really hard not to behave badly in this way again. Finally, you must resolve to try and perform only positive and virtuous actions from now on.

what you do, you remember

A useful way to think about purifying negative karma is in terms of its effect on your consciousness. If you have done something you know is wrong – even if this was a long time ago – feelings of guilt will lurk somewhere in the unconscious depths of your mind and cause discomfort and suffering to arise from time to time. To put it simply, what you do, you remember. When the memory of a negative action surfaces in your consciousness, the fear, anxiety and worry that simultaneously arise are a karmic result of this unenlightened behaviour.

So if you do something kind, generous or compassionate, the memory makes you feel happy, but if you do something mean and nasty, you also

have to remember that and the memory will make you feel quite
different. Because these latter memories are unpleasant, you try to
repress them or run away from them, or get caught up in other unskilful
behaviour; this is part of the karmic result too. So it is not only your
negative actions that you purify, but also the state of mind underlying the
mistaken action — in other words, you purify your negative thinking.

When memories of past behaviour surface in the mind, they can be regarded partly as karmic consequences of those actions.

behavioural patterns

In a similar way to musical talent being the karmic result of musical training
in an earlier life (see page 43), you can also see behavioural patterns as
karmic results. For instance, if someone tends to get angry easily, this can
be seen as a karmic consequence of previous angry behaviour that he or

she now has the opportunity to try and purify. This person needs to try hard, and sincerely, not to give in to the impulse to be angry, by reflecting that anger will only create negative karma for himself or herself.

One of the laws of karma is that the result of any action increases over time, in the same way that one fruit seed grows into a tree and makes many fruits. This is an incentive to purify your mind so that you do not commit negative actions again, as well as purifying the karmic potential from your previous negative actions. Whenever you are tempted to put off purifying negative actions, thinking there is no harm in leaving them for a while, you can remind yourself that the longer you leave it, the greater your negative karma will be. If you do not purify your negative karma in this life, then it will carry over to the next rebirth and manifest more strongly.

taking appropriate counteraction

Alongside purification of the negative karma of an unskilful action, you also need to cultivate positive karma from a skilful action of a similar nature. For example, imagine a person who habitually used to practise theft, but has now resolved to abandon such unskilful actions, through experiencing the unfortunate results of negative karmic consequences. The best counteractive action in this particular case is to cultivate positive karma by acts of generosity and giving. The person should practise these skilful actions whenever possible, and even search out opportunities to give his or her possessions away.

When you first acknowledge that you have done many wrong actions throughout your current and past lives, it is easy to fall into the trap of low self-esteem. You can end up feeling that everything is hopeless. However, you do not have to self-identify with your negative behaviour. If you start feeling depressed about your previous bad actions and their consequences, then you can recall the many positive actions you have also done. The essence of purification is simply to let go of your problems and mistakes by seeing them as temporary blips on your stream of consciousness, not as an intrinsic part of your nature. By not identifying with your problems and mistakes, and by seeing their transitory nature, you will find them less difficult to deal with and easier to let go of and purify.

clearing karmic potential

Karmic potential – both good and bad – can only be erased from the depths of the unconscious mind in one of two ways. There are no other possibilities for karmic potential because the seeds have already been sown through actions. So the karma either comes to fruition in a given situation, or is purified with one of the appropriate countermeasures. Except for these two cases, karmic potential remains somewhere in the mental continuum until the right conditions arise for the karma to manifest, or until it is purified beforehand if the person undertakes appropriate positive action.

A simple purification ritual of burning incense is a powerful symbol of clearing negative karma, and is a useful practice to accompany meditation. Take one or several sticks of incense and light them mindfully. Clasp the lighted incense in your hands, which should be held in the prayer gesture (see page 108): first above your head, then in turn at your throat and heart. This represents clearing negative karma of body, speech and mind. Then place the incense on your altar and you are ready to begin your meditation session.

Burning incense in a simple ritual before you meditate can be a powerful way of helping purify negative karma.

Milarepa cups his ear with his right hand in the gesture of singing. His left hand holds a skullcup of nectar.

case study: the life of Milarepa

The 12th-century Tibetan Buddhist yogi and poet Jetsun Milarepa is famous for his songs of joyous inspiration on the Buddhist path. He is revered particularly for his enduring perseverance and his determination in the spiritual quest for enlightenment, despite enormous hardships imposed by his teacher, Marpa.

Among Tibetan Buddhists, Milarepa's marvellous reputation for meditation and spiritual practice is almost without equal. Yet in his earlier life Milarepa committed many grievous misdeeds. His story shows the incredible power of purification practices to transform even terrible negative karma into a dedicated spirituality that eventually led to full and perfect awakening in only one lifetime.

the art of black magic

When Milarepa was about seven years old his father died, entrusting his widow, children and estate into the care of his brother and sister-in-law. However, they took everything of value for themselves and caused much hardship to Milarepa's family. As a result of this brutal, unfair behaviour, Milarepa learnt the art of black magic in order to take revenge on his relatives on behalf of his mother, who had been so grievously wronged. He used his powers to create a hailstorm that caused the death of several relatives and other people and the destruction of a house, and during this maelstrom some birds and animals also died.

Some time after this devastation, Milarepa understood the gravity of his actions and their karmic consequences and decided to try and purify his negative karma. Determined to right his wrongs, he set off in search of a spiritual teacher who could help him. After spending time with one teacher, he heard about the wonderful master Marpa the Translator and set off to meet him. Milarepa repented and regretted his previous bad ways and placed himself under his teacher's instruction.

the trials of Milarepa

Marpa realized the gravity of Milarepa's situation and put him through terrible trials, which served as purification practices. These hardships mainly involved Milarepa building many houses for his teacher, which Marpa insisted he do before he would give Milarepa any Buddhist teachings. The building work was tough because Milarepa had to hew stones and carry them long distances, as well as constructing the houses. However, this hardship seemed slight when Marpa then made him pull the houses down and take the materials back to where they had come from. Marpa even threw Milarepa off a tall tower that he had built for him.

Such apparently appalling actions do not appear to be the behaviour of an enlightened teacher, but Marpa knew what suffering Milarepa must endure in order to purify all his negative karma. So Marpa's actions were actually a great kindness to Milarepa, allowing him to purify his negative acts in the same lifetime they were committed. Milarepa then spent many years meditating in a cave, eating only nettles, and attracted numerous devotees and eventually attained enlightenment.

a meditation on the nature of suffering

The main point in this meditation is to become aware of how much dissatisfaction and suffering exist every day in this world, both for you and for others.

The meditation usually refers to suffering rather than dissatisfaction, but includes all levels of not being happy – such as mild dissatisfaction, suffering and absolute anguish – and refers to all states of being: physical, emotional and mental. You might wonder why you should meditate on the nature of suffering, as this must be unpleasant, but this meditation helps you develop a more realistic understanding of life. Accepting the existence of dissatisfaction, rather than fighting against it, helps to prevent causing negative karma and more suffering.

1 Sit comfortably with your back straight. Close your eyes and bring your attention to your breath. Observe your breathing for a few minutes to calm the mind.

2 The first aspect of dissatisfaction, or suffering, is the pain of suffering. This includes all forms of easily noticed suffering, such as physical pain, mental turmoil and emotional distress. Contemplate physical suffering, and remember times when you were in extreme pain. Think about how many little aches and pains you experience throughout each day. Reflect that this discomfort will only worsen as you get older, and consider how unwise it is to be attached to your body.

3 Contemplate emotional and mental suffering. Think of all the times when you have been lonely, depressed, jealous, anxious and angry. There has hardly been a time when you felt no emotional or mental pain at all. Reflect that everyone – just like you – wants to be happy and avoid suffering. Dissatisfaction is universal, not personal.

4 The second aspect is the suffering of change. This is subtler, as it concerns things that we think bring us happiness. Reflect on the saying 'All good things come to an end'. Contemplate all the wonderful experiences and objects you have had: special holidays, loving relationships, great sex, fast cars and beautiful clothes. When they are over, you miss them, and this causes dissatisfaction.

5 Everything changes, and clinging to pleasure inevitably brings pain. Beauty fades, youth turns to old age and eventually death, and money is spent. None of these things can bring lasting happiness.

6 The third aspect is all-pervasive suffering. This refers to the very nature of our existence, and how we foolishly believe we can find happiness in temporal, transient things, while trying to forget the suffering of sickness and death. The Buddhist path offers ways to lessen suffering, and eventually remove the causes for dissatisfaction altogether. But it is important first to acknowledge and understand the painful nature of existence.

7 Resolve to become less attached to things and accept that they will change. Think how everyone else is also caught up in dissatisfaction, and resolve to be kind to others as much as possible.

transforming adversity and cultivating wisdom

The wonderful story below shows that transforming adversity can be as simple as thinking about it differently.

An invading army arrived in a small town ready to kill anyone who resisted them. Most people immediately surrendered or fled. The army general strode arrogantly into the Buddhist temple and encountered a Zen priest. Annoyed that the priest showed no fear and did not immediately fall to the ground begging for his life, the general waved his sword menacingly and yelled, 'Don't you know that you are looking at a man who could run you through without blinking?' The priest replied calmly, 'And you, sir, are looking at a man who can be run through without blinking.' The general had no answer to the priest's unexpected reply, so he bowed respectfully and left.

thinking differently

When things go wrong, it is easy to become depressed, angry or hopeless. However, if you regard these misfortunes as opportunities for change, by cultivating wisdom and applying effort you can transform the way you deal with unfortunate circumstances. You can't stop bad things happening – they are a part of life – but you can change your responses. Because you cannot alter the adverse circumstances themselves, you are faced with transforming your negative feelings: the passions of anger, hatred and aversion. As these are so strong, this is not easy, but by practising moral restraint, patience and wisdom, you can gradually change negative emotions.

When you are faced with adverse circumstances, feeling unhappy serves no purpose in overcoming the undesirable situation. It is not only futile, but aggravates your own anxiety and brings about a dissatisfied state of mind. Use your wisdom to reason whether anything can be done to resolve the adverse circumstances. If resolution is possible, there is no need to worry; and if nothing can be done, it is pointless to worry. Either way, worrying is a waste of time. The wise response is to be patient in the face of adversity; this not only prevents you acting out of anger and creating negative karma, but also lessens your suffering.

points of view are ephemeral

Next time suffering arises, reflect that this is a wonderful opportunity to use wisdom and purify some of your negative karma created from an earlier unskilful action. For instance, arguments often arise over two different points of view. Remember that points of view are ephemeral; they have no inherent existence, because a point of view is simply one person's perception. Thinking like this helps let go of attachment to your own point of view. Usually the argument can then swiftly be resolved. So instead of feeling trapped by a difficult situation, regard it as an opportunity to break free from your habitual thought and behavioural patterns. Letting the other person have their way is a sign of strength and wisdom, not weakness.

how to do cow-face pose

Gomukasana, or cow-face pose, releases tension and helps you achieve calmness.

Sit with your legs outstretched, then bend your left leg under your right leg, and place your left ankle by your right hip. Then cross your right leg over your left. Raise your left arm over your head and down, and move your right arm behind your back and up. Clasp your two hands together behind your left shoulder. Stay in the pose for up to 60 seconds, then repeat on the other side.

karma and psychology

You can use your inner psychological faculties to investigate what causes you to think and act in the way you do, and thereby develop a greater understanding of karma.

For instance, by contemplating and analyzing cause and effect, you can develop a reasoned, logical understanding that the teachings on karma are correct. In this way you go beyond the superstitions of blind faith, so that if you – or even someone else – question your understanding of, or belief in, karma, you can respond with the conviction of sound reasoning and valid arguments. A developed psychological understanding of karma also leads you naturally towards positive, skilful actions.

Manjushri, the Tibetan bodhisattva of wisdom, wields a flaming sword and a lotus bearing a Buddhist text.

using your inner wisdom

However, if you do not use your wonderful psychological ability to investigate, analyze and reflect, then even if you have a great mental and intellectual capacity, it will remain undeveloped. From a Buddhist perspective, psychological understanding includes using your inner wisdom. Inner wisdom relies partly on intellect, but it is much more than intellectual understanding; it is a special kind of knowing – the inexplicable sense of intimacy that comes with experience.

Each time you meditate you can also use your psychological faculties to further develop your understanding of karma. However, eventually this process will reveal that no matter how long you contemplate a subject such as karma and enquire into its nature, sometimes you must accept that you have only a limited understanding. You will reach a point where, however much psychological enquiry and meditation you have done, aspects of karma remain that you simply do not know.

dreams and archetypes

The great pioneer of psychology, Carl Jung, realized that not everything can be consciously known or understood, because some things reside in the unconscious mind. As you read earlier, dreams partly function to bring 'stuff' through from the unconscious to consciousness. Archetypes, or powerful universal symbols, also impact on both the unconscious and conscious minds. If you continue meditating regularly, you can begin to understand more of the insights that arise from contemplation and enquiry. But sometimes it is best to accept that you simply do not know everything in a rational, conscious manner, but that insights may come through to consciousness from the unconscious mind.

Meditation can lead to an intuitive experiential understanding, which facilitates a shift in perception. This allows you to realize that meditation is no longer an intellectual process; you can go beyond the intellect and access deeper levels of the mind. When you meditate on karma in this way, your understanding of intentional actions and their results deepens, and a deeper understanding of how karma operates begins to arise. You start to know for yourself the truth of karma, but this is an understanding that arises from your direct personal experience, not from something you read in a book.

Reciting prayers and affirmations with sincerity helps to purify negative thoughts and train the mind to think positively.

affirmations and prayers for good karma

The following affirmations and prayers can be recited at the beginning or end of a meditation session, or read and reflected upon informally at any time.

The prayers are drawn from traditional Buddhist texts, and have been used extensively over the centuries to help train the mind to think positively and altruistically. Affirmations are a modern equivalent of traditional prayers, and offer a similar contemporary method of cultivating positive thoughts and discouraging negative ones. Both prayers and affirmations help to purify negative thinking, and lead the mind towards initiating only positive intentional actions.

suggested recitations

The sincere and regular recitation of both prayers and affirmations creates good karma.

- May all living beings have happiness and the causes of happiness.
  May all living beings be free from suffering and the causes of suffering.
  May all living beings never be separated from the happiness that knows no suffering.
  May all living beings abide in equanimity, free from attachment and anger that hold some close and others distant.

- To give meaning to my life and create good karma, I envisage my heart as a temple of love from which I reach out to others with compassion and wisdom.
  My moral values are to love and respect all others, whoever they may be.

- I believe in universal responsibility to all other living beings. I know that whatever I do matters and has a karmic effect on the rest of the world.

- For as long as space endures
  And for as long as living beings remain,
  Until then may I too abide,
  To dispel the misery of the world.

- Through each virtuous action I undertake may I quickly purify my negative karma, and through being of benefit to other beings may I quickly create positive karma.

- If I practise unselfishness and generosity, greed and avarice will become less and I will create good karma.
  If I practise love and kindness, anger and hatred will vanish and I will create good karma.
  If I develop wisdom and knowledge, ignorance and delusion will gradually disappear and I will purify my negative karma.

- Restraining myself and loving others creates positive karmic seeds that will bear fruit in this life and beyond.

- It is more important to examine my own actions, and see where I can make improvements, than to criticize the actions of others.

- The mind that is free from the delusions of desire, hatred, anger and ignorance knows instinctively when and how to act for the greatest good.
  Therefore, I will cultivate a mind that is free of these delusions, in order for good karma to blossom and for negative karma to fade away.

- Actions that lead not to distress,
  But to a heart bright and cheerful,
  Are good karma.
  Knowing this good karma is useful,
  I should act quickly thereon.

karmic insights from astrology, tarot and I Ching

The ancient divination arts of astrology, tarot cards and the I Ching, or Book of Changes, are most commonly used in the contemporary world for some kind of prediction purposes.

For example, perhaps you visit an astrologer or study your horoscope yourself, to try to understand what the planetary alignments at your birth might mean and whether they can shed any light on your future life. Many people – even those who don't 'believe' in astrology – read (often somewhat furtively) their horoscope in the papers, to see what astrologers have predicted might happen to them in the future.

Tarot cards are laid out in one of several traditional formations. The pattern of the cards is then 'read' for divination.

Other people might use a set of tarot cards or throw coins and then consult the I Ching for the similar purpose of trying to see what the future potentially holds. Many different sets of tarot cards are available these days, but they all have the same format, with each card having a symbolic picture with a title. You could start by using one of the original versions, such as the Waite or Crowley packs. The cards are laid out in one of several traditional formations, and then either a tarot card reader or you yourself 'read' what each card might mean in that particular place, and what the overall impression might be.

the Book of Changes

In the I Ching, or Book of Changes, throwing coins is used as a method of divination. With each throw, the combination of heads and tails determines whether the resulting line is broken or unbroken. Three coins are thrown six times to create two sets of trigrams (three lines), which are placed one above the other to make a six-line configuration. Originally a set of small sticks or straws was thrown, but these days people generally use coins. Once you have noted down the six lines, you refer to the table of trigrams to find which two trigrams you have thrown. You then turn to the appropriate section of the book and read the cryptic passage that represents the two trigrams.

There is nothing wrong with acting out this natural urge to try to divine your possible future – and as long as your intention is skilful, such actions do not create bad karma. However, there is perhaps a deeper, more profound way of using these divination tools that might allow you to gain insight into the way karma has affected your present situation and how it might affect your karmic potential.

motivation

From the perspective of gaining karmic insight, the most useful approach to astrology, tarot and I Ching is to examine your motivation for wishing to explore these divination tools in the first place. For many people, idle curiosity might be their starting point, perhaps choosing to turn to the horoscope page in their newspaper. However, this mild interest can lead to a more profound journey into what can be learnt from one of these divination arts. Approaching them with the motivation of wishing to gain insight into your current situation and personality, in order to deepen your understanding of yourself, can be helpful on the spiritual path.

The different trigrams of the I Ching are arrived at by throwing coins, and then one trigram is placed above the other.

Chi'en   K'un   Chen   K'an

Ken   Sun   Li   Tui

Chi Kung exercise for inner strength

The following exercise for developing inner strength is drawn from Chi Kung, the ancient Chinese system of rhythmic movements for promoting the harmonious flow of subtle energies, known collectively as chi, throughout mind, body and spirit. The movements gently stimulate and strengthen your subtle energies and are traditionally performed in time with the breath. This exercise helps you draw in fresh, new chi to recharge your resources of subtle energy and develop inner strength. The benefits of performing this exercise include enhanced concentration, stress reduction and a relaxed, strengthened nervous system.

1 Stand with your feet apart, slightly wider than your hips, and make sure your arms are hanging loosely at your sides. Keep your palms facing inwards and gently touching your thighs. Check to make sure your knees are soft, relaxed and slightly bent. Exhale fully, emptying your lungs.

2 Take a long, deep inhalation, and slowly raise your arms upwards and out to the sides. Keep your arms soft and naturally rounded, and make sure your feet are firmly on the ground. Look straight ahead, as if at a distant horizon, to keep yourself grounded and balanced.

3 Continue raising your arms until they are above your head. Make sure you keep them relaxed and soft at all times, to promote the easy flow of new chi energy.

Continue to inhale deeply to absorb the rising chi energy generated by the movement of your arms and the expansion of your chest.

4 When your arms are above your body and slightly more than shoulder-width apart, hold them still in this position. Visualize chi energy filling your palms from the sunlight above. Try to imagine that your hands are like sponges, absorbing chi energy through the palms. Stand and absorb new chi like this for a few breaths, keeping your inhalations and exhalations deep and long. When you feel ready, exhale and bring your arms gently down over the top of your head, in front of your body.

5 As you move your arms down, you naturally bring the chi into your body, through your face, chest and abdomen. Imagine the new chi energy sweeping down your body, calming and relaxing you, and clearing away any stagnant old chi. Keep your palms facing in towards your body as you move them slowly downwards.

6 As you gradually finish the out-breath, gently lower your head and relax your jaw as your hands continue downwards to the top of your thighs. You may like to repeat the exercise a few times, in which case start again from the beginning. When you are ready to finish, simply move on into your normal daily life. You should feel strong, recharged and relaxed.

DISCOVERING YOUR KARMIC PURPOSE IN LIFE

Understanding how karma operates is the first step towards transforming your life, and this transformation is the key to discovering real happiness by awakening to your true nature. In this chapter you will read about the importance of transforming your behaviour in a way that creates happiness and avoids suffering – the spiritual path that leads to Nirvana, the ultimate purpose of life. Awakening to your true nature does not mean learning something new or adopting a new philosophy. Awakening is the inner process of letting go of your wrong views and unskilful actions – the total abandonment of ignorance, hatred, anger, desire, attachment and aversion – until your true nature is revealed.

The Wheel of Life illustrates the Buddhist teachings on cyclic existence as a motivation to try to awaken. At the centre are a pig, a cockerel and a snake, symbolizing the Three Poisons of ignorance, desire and aversion. The outer ring depicts the 12 links of dependent origination, and the whole wheel is clasped in the jaws of a red demon symbolizing impermanence.

nirvana: the Buddhist philosophy of awakening

Nirvana is also referred to as awakening, enlightenment or liberation. Awakening is perhaps the best word to describe this elusive state that the Buddha experienced, because *budh* – the root of the word Buddha – means to awaken.

Awakening usually takes many lifetimes of dedicated practice and meditation, but it is not impossible. Any being can – eventually – awaken; the Buddha's life is an example of someone who awakened. A brief look at his life reveals the path to awakening, and is an inspiration to follow this path too.

the life of the Buddha

Prince Siddhartha was born about 2,500 years ago into a royal family in north India. At the ceremony celebrating his birth a famous soothsayer predicted that he would either be a great king or a great religious leader. This revelation seriously concerned the king, who wished his son to inherit and rule the kingdom after his death. So he decided that his son would have no opportunities for spiritual enquiry, by confining Siddhartha to the palace and keeping him occupied with pleasure and satisfying his desires.

Siddhartha's early years were spent surrounded by luxury and beauty, his every wish granted as soon as it was known. One day, bored with pleasure, he realized he had never stepped outside the palace walls, and wondered about the world beyond his life of luxurious confinement. The king reluctantly arranged for Siddhartha to visit the local town, but ordered his servants to keep the unpleasant facts of life away from the prince. Despite these precautions, Siddhartha saw an old person, a sick person and a corpse. These sights troubled him deeply, as he realized that all beings (including himself) would inevitably experience the pains and sorrows of old age, sickness and death.

Siddhartha wandered despondently down to the river to reflect on this awful new discovery. On the way he saw a holy man, wearing only rags and with few possessions, but radiating immense happiness and inner peace. Siddhartha then realized there was a way out of the suffering of existence that he had just witnessed. He fled the palace that night and joined the wandering holy men, learning meditation and religious philosophy. After many years of diligent meditation and practising the ascetic's life of austerity, Siddhartha understood he had learnt many beneficial spiritual techniques, but had not yet resolved the issue of the suffering of the human condition.

Buddha's awakening

He sat down under a tree to meditate, and resolved not to get up until he had awakened. For seven days Siddhartha sat in deep meditation and experienced the arising of fear and desire, but by seeing them as transitory illusions and distractions he remained steadfast in his meditation. On the dawn of the eighth day, as the light of the morning star filtered through the leaves, he finally attained Nirvana. He had become the Buddha and realized the Four Noble Truths: that suffering exists, that the cause of suffering is craving, that there is an end to suffering, and that there is a path that leads to the end of suffering and towards awakening.

The Buddha was an ordinary human being, like us, and just as Buddha finally awakened to his true nature, so we all have the same potential. This potential is called Buddha nature, and everyone – even animals – has Buddha nature and can eventually awaken. Buddha taught his disciples about love, wisdom and compassion, and about karma: the importance of recognizing that their own actions brought suffering or happiness, depending on their motivation.

Everyone reading this book has already created the good karma to have the opportunity to progress towards Nirvana, but in order to awaken you must practise meditation and morality. To protect the good karma you have now, and to create more positive karma in order to be able to continue on the path to awakening, you need to act skilfully, with wisdom and compassion.

Regular sessions of meditation, combined with altruistic acts of love, wisdom and compassion, leads you gradually towards awakening.

cooling the passion of craving

Awakening is letting go of all desires, cravings and wishes that things were different; it can be described as cooling the passion of craving. It might not sound much fun, because we mistakenly believe that if we get what we crave, we will be happy. But awakening is the realization that there will always be something else to crave – the state of perpetual unfulfilment that is suffering – and so abandoning craving altogether really is the path to true happiness.

Buddhas – awakened ones – do not turn their backs on the suffering of others. They live in the midst of the world to respond to the needs of others with wisdom and compassion. They often lead simple lives with few possessions, yet radiate contentment. Those who have awakened have gone beyond karma altogether, so they do not even have the desire to create good karma from their altruistic acts; compassion is simply their natural response to others.

Awakening is not something to attain – it is an inner realization, and the cessation of craving. Although awakening can take many lifetimes, when the moment comes you understand that Buddha nature was there all along; you simply did not realize it. It is said that when the moment of awakening occurs, the person often laughs because it now seems so obvious; life has not changed, but it is seen in a different, awakened way.

the path to Nirvana

The teachings on karma can help you take the first steps on the path to awakening. Continually reminding yourself that all actions create karma helps you to be mindful of your behaviour. You know that bad actions motivated by selfishness, anger, hatred and craving will produce bad karma and will keep you trapped in suffering. However, good actions motivated by altruism, compassion and wisdom will create good karma and happiness, and will lead down the path to Nirvana.

the Buddha's eight-step path to awakening

As you have just read, awakening to your true nature – attaining Nirvana – is not easy, and usually takes many lifetimes. You need to free yourself completely from the desire for and attachment to things you like, and from an aversion to and hatred of what you don't like.

The best way to find Nirvana is to follow Buddha's Noble Eightfold Path, a guide to living well that is designed to help you awaken eventually. The Noble Eightfold Path is the fourth Noble Truth mentioned earlier, the path that leads to the cessation of suffering. It comprises: Right View, Right Thought, Right Speech, Right Action, Right Livelihood, Right Effort, Right Mindfulness and Right Concentration.

Being mindful not to kill insects and other animals when you garden is an example of Right Action.

the Noble Eightfold Path

The eight points of the path are defined under three categories: wisdom, morality and meditation. These three need to be cultivated together; you are not supposed to learn or practise them in a linear sequence. Wisdom, morality and meditation reinforce each other – the sum of them is greater than the individual parts. Wisdom includes Right View and Right Thought; morality includes Right Speech, Right Action, Right Livelihood and Right Effort; and meditation includes Right Mindfulness and Right Concentration.

- Right View is the foundation of the Buddhist path, the first step, which is to understand that suffering permeates existence, but there is a way out. Then you must try out the steps on the path, which Buddha taught leads to awakening. If you do not test his teachings in your own life, you are taking them on trust, which is blind faith – something Buddha discouraged. Our views shape our perceptions and establish our values; they create a framework through which we interpret the world and the meaning of existence. Buddha taught that there were two distinct views: Wrong View, which leads towards actions that cause suffering; and Right View, which guides us towards Right Action, and ultimately towards awakening.

- Right Thought is about developing good motivation and good intention. It helps you change your habitual self-centred thinking and has three aspects. Renunciation arises from understanding suffering and its causes, and is the abandoning of desire and attachment. This encourages a natural goodwill towards others, because you understand that they too live lives permeated by suffering and wish to find happiness. This inclines you towards harmlessness, and the wish that all beings be free from suffering. You can train your mind by trying to substitute Right Thought for negative thoughts whenever they arise in your mind.

- Right Speech includes not lying, and trying always to be truthful; not slandering others, and cultivating speech that promotes friendship and harmony; not shouting angry abuse, and cultivating courteous, friendly speech; not gossiping or speaking mindlessly, and cultivating valuable, important speech. Right Speech is an encouragement to think before you speak, to check your intention and motivation. It relies on being mindful whenever you speak, and being careful that what you say promotes happiness and avoids causing suffering.

- Right Action is thoughtful behaviour that does not harm others, and the Buddhist teachings on karma are a good guide to Right Action. Not killing includes respecting the right for all beings to live their lives trying to find happiness. You can refrain from mindlessly killing insects by remembering that all living beings have Buddha nature. Not stealing includes cultivating honesty and respect for the possessions of others, and being satisfied with what you have. Not misusing the senses means not over-indulging in sensual gratification, and appreciating the value of moderation. Not misusing intoxicants means abstention from (or moderate intake of) alcohol and similar substances, so as to prevent mindless intoxicated behaviour that causes suffering.

- Right Livelihood has already been explored in some depth in the chapter on karma and your career (see page 58). Essentially it means making a living in an ethical way. Because modern society often encourages the making of a profit at the expense of ethics, you need to choose your job carefully. Buddha taught that money should only be earnt legally, non-violently, harmlessly and honestly. Useful jobs that help others are the ideal expression of Right Livelihood, but at the very least you can avoid working for companies that trade in arms, pollutants and the suffering of humans or animals.

- Right Effort is not about trying to make something particular happen. It is about trying to be aware and mindful from moment to moment, and endeavouring to overcome the laziness and negative behaviour that cause suffering and bad karma. Right Effort involves energy, which can be directed in positive ways, such as generosity and compassion, or negatively in anger and desire. So Right Effort involves trying to direct your energy towards wholesome states of mind and actions. Buddha stressed the need for exertion and perseverance; he showed us the path to awakening, but it is up to us to follow it.

- Right Mindfulness is integral to meditation and facilitates the attainment of serenity and insight. The opposite of mindfulness is mindlessness, where you don't think about the consequences of what you say or do, which can cause bad karma and suffering. Mindfulness trains you to be present in the moment, observing what arises without leaping to judgement and reaction. Living attentively with your bare experience is Right Mindfulness, as is avoiding desire, idle dreams and rigid thoughts.

- Right Concentration in meditation develops a single pointed mind, where you remain calm and focused. Buddha taught that the ultimate purpose of Right Concentration is developing wisdom, the remedy for ignorance, which is the basis for all suffering. Right Concentration returns us to Right View at a higher level, because our fundamental misperception of how we exist – as independent beings, rather than interdependently with others – obscures wisdom. Each point on the Noble Eightfold Path gradually purifies your mental continuum and leads you towards Nirvana.

Working in one of the caring professions, such as being a nurse or a doctor, is a good expression of Right Livelihood.

a meditation on finding true happiness

This meditation helps you realize your great good fortune at being born a human and having the opportunity to learn about karma and other Buddhist teachings. Meditating on the precious nature of human life helps you discover true happiness, and is a good way to dispel negative emotions. The meditation encourages you to look at and clearly recognize all the many good things you have in your life, and helps you feel grateful and joyful about your good fortune, as well as feeling compassion for other less fortunate beings.

1 Sit comfortably with your back straight. Close your eyes and bring your attention to your breath. Observe your breathing for a few minutes to calm the mind.

2 Assess how you feel. Go beyond your usual superficial responses, and enquire deeply into your feelings about yourself. Most of us have ambiguous feelings: we feel positive about some aspects of ourselves, but also hold negative emotions, such as depression, feelings of inadequacy and hopelessness. Even if you feel positive and happy now, acknowledge that you do sometimes feel negative and low, and determine to transform all your negative feelings and find true happiness.

3 Think about what it would be like to be an animal, completely at the mercy of your desires. Unlike humans, animals have no opportunity for the spiritual development that facilitates finding true happiness. Reflect how fearful of humans most wild animals and birds are. Imagine what it would be like to live in this constant state of fear and paranoia.

4 Bring to mind how people living in extreme poverty might feel. Their lives are characterized by constant hunger, which they have no ability to relieve. They live in dreadful circumstances, without easy access to clean water, shelter or medicine. Such people often have to beg, and suffer abuse from other people. Imagine how it would be to live like this.

5 Bring to mind your own problems and see how minor they seem in comparison. Realize how insignificant your difficulties are in this broader context. Feel thankful for the opportunities and comforts you have in your life, and generate compassion for those who are less fortunate.

6 Reflect upon your advantages, and appreciate your good fortune. You have friends and family who love you, opportunities for education, travel, relationships and work. You have enough to eat, a home, access to doctors and medicine, and many other benefits. Most importantly you have an intelligent mind, the opportunity to learn about the Buddhist teachings and to meditate, and the possibility of transforming suffering and finding true happiness.

7 Allow your mind to rest in appreciation of the many good things in your life. Feel happy for yourself, and compassion for those less fortunate than you. Finally, wish that all beings might find true happiness and avoid suffering.

how to do corpse pose

Savasana, or corpse pose, is always done at the end of
your yoga practice and also represents the end of the
spiritual path: Nirvana.

Lie on your back, with your feet slightly apart
and your arms a little way from your sides.
Relax your whole body. Close your eyes and
bring your attention to your breath. As
thoughts arise, let them go, and return to
the breath until your mind is calm. Rest
like this for up to ten minutes.

index

Acknowledgements

Executive Editor Sandra Rigby
Editor Emma Pattison
Executive Art Editor Sally Bond
Designer Annika Skoog and Claire Oldman for Cobalt I D
Illustrator Robert Beer
Picture Research Emma O'Neill
Production Manager Louise Hall

Special Photography © Octopus Publishing Group Limited/Paul Bricknell.

Other photography: Alamy/Carles O. Cecil 61; /Paul Lovichi 10. Banana Stock 85. Robert Beer 69, 90, 100, 106, 117. Bridgeman Art Library/Museum of Fine Arts, Boston, Massachusetts, USA 46-47. Corbis UK Limited 14, 52; /Keren Su 8. Garden Picture Library/Matthew Wakem 39. Getty Images/Theodore Anderson 40; /Daryl Benson 44; /Richard Drury 120; /Diana Healey 82; /G & M David de Lossy 57; /Marcus Mok 43; /Peter Nicholson 98; /Jose Luis Pelaez 123; /Stuart O'Sullivan 22; /Upperhall Ltd 58; /Roger Viollet 16. Image Source 11, 21, 97. Octopus Publishing Group Limited 42; /Peter Pugh-Cook 112, 113; /Russell Sadur 26. PhotoDisc 2, 13, 78. Photolibrary Group 110. Photofusion Picture Library/Martin Bond 54.